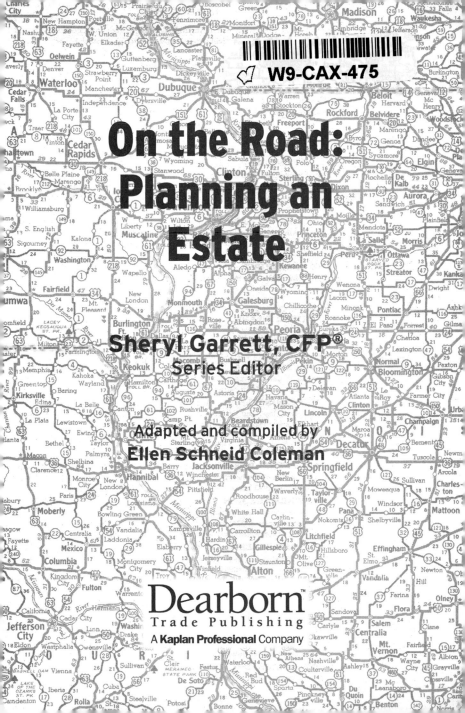

W9-CAX-475

On the Road: Planning an Estate

Sheryl Garrett, CFP®
Series Editor

Adapted and compiled by
Ellen Schneid Coleman

Dearborn™
Trade Publishing

A **Kaplan Professional** Company

This publication is designed to provide accurate and authoritative information in regard to the subject matter covered. It is sold with the understanding that the publisher is not engaged in rendering legal, accounting, or other professional service. If legal advice or other expert assistance is required, the services of a competent professional person should be sought.

President, Dearborn Publishing: Roy Lipner
Vice President and Publisher: Cynthia A. Zigmund
Senior Acquisitions Editor: Mary B. Good
Cover Design: Design Solutions

Published by Dearborn Trade Publishing
A Kaplan Professional Company

A Stonesong Press Book

Project Manager: Ellen Schneid Coleman
Interior Design: Brad Walrod/High Text Graphics, Inc.

Printed in the United States of America

06 07 08   10 9 8 7 6 5 4 3 2 1

Library of Congress Cataloging-in-Publication Data
Planning an estate/edited by Sheryl Garrett; adapted and
compiled by Ellen Schneid Coleman.
 p. cm.—(On the road)
 Includes index.
 ISBN 1-4195-0044-9 (5 × 7.375 pbk.)
 1. Estate planning—United States.   I. Garrett, Sheryl.   II. Coleman,
Ellen Schneid.   III. On the road (Chicago, Ill.)
KF750.Z9O5 2006
346.7305'2—dc22   2005021738

Contents

Introduction

On the Road: Planning an Estate is part of a new series of books from Dearborn Trade Publishing intended to help you deal with the financial issues, problems, and decisions concerning specific life events. The decisions you face when you're about to plan your estate are similar to those you have to make when you decide to get married or to create a financial plan. In fact, despite what people often think, estate planning is not just for the 50 plus crowd; it's for anyone with assets or loved ones to protect. And that means you, if you're just starting a first job and building a 401(k), a new mom or dad, an owner of a new home or condo, or about to retire and enjoy your hard-earned assets. Here are some of the things you should consider whether this is your first or tenth time preparing a plan (yes, your plan should be reviewed and revised periodically as your circumstances change):

▶ Do you have a written estate plan?
▶ Do you have a will?
▶ Have you considered a living trust to avoid probate?
▶ Have you delegated appropriate powers of attorney so that, if necessary, your affairs can be managed by people you choose?
▶ Are you taking full advantage of the marital deduction?
▶ Have you set up irrevocable life insurance trusts to ensure your life insurance proceeds are not taxed as part of your estate?
▶ Are you taking maximum advantage of the $11,000 annual gift tax exclusions?
▶ Are you taking maximum advantage of medical and education gift tax exclusions?
▶ If you have highly appreciated assets that don't generate current income, have you considered using them to fund a charitable remainder trust?
▶ If you are a business owner, have you protected it?

Financial planning shouldn't be intimidating. That's why we've created these books to take away the terror. On the Road books are like travel guides, which will help you make the best financial decisions at each stage of your life—in this case, when you are ready to do some estate planning. In this book we'll address the questions that concern you as you are about to embark down the road toward planning your estate.

These financial decisions are part of your life's journey, so we've made them easy to navigate, with lots of helpful "Roadmaps" (charts and tables of financial information to help you with each issue or decision that comes up) and "Tollbooths" that help you calculate your expenses or savings, as well as "Hazard" signs that caution you on money pitfalls to watch out for. We even tell you "What To Pack" so that you'll know what forms or other information you need to write a will or add a codicil, for example. We've made sure you know what we're talking about, by providing "Learn the Language" definitions of unfamiliar or technical terms particular to each estate planning topic.

And we've included "Postcards" that tell helpful stories of how other people have made their estate planning journey successfully.

Finally, we've included an "Itinerary," a recap of all the key actions you should take—all of which is discussed in detail in the seven chapters of this book. You can use this as a handy reminder at each stage of your journey toward estate planning. At the end we have included a list of other books and resources you could turn to if you want more in-depth information on any aspect of estate planning.

We hope you find this "travel" guide helpful as you map your route to financial success and peace of mind. Life is an adventure, and money paves the way. So let's get started on the road: the light is green, put your pedal to the metal, and go!

Design Your Itinerary

The Fundamentals of Estate Planning

▶ Where Are You Now?

Let's face a fact: We will all die someday. Thinking about it may make you uncomfortable, but you will die someday and you need to prepare for it now. You have sweated and toiled to own a home or stash some cash in bank accounts and invested in the stock market or in retirement plans. When death knocks at your door, you sure want all this to go to the right person, people, or causes. When that unfortunate event occurs, whether it is tomorrow or decades from now, your assets will be distributed, and your estate may have to pay estate taxes. What you should decide now is whether you want to control how your estate is settled or leave it up to the probate court, which might distribute your property in a manner that would not please you if you were alive.

When you hear the word estate, you may envision something big and grandiose and far beyond your own financial reality—a mansion, for example. However, in the eyes of the law, your estate is simply everything you own, by yourself or with others. Your home, car, furniture, bank accounts, jewelry, life insurance policy, retirement plan, stocks and bonds, and other assets are all part of your estate. Although some people have large estates worth millions, most Americans have relatively modest estates.

If you ignore the process of estate planning, you not only lose control of how your worldly possessions will be handed out, but your estate might pay thousands of dollars in estate taxes that could easily have been avoided. (In some states, if you die without a will, most of your assets go to your children, with only a small remainder left for your surviving spouse.)

On the other hand, if you make the effort to maximize basic estate planning techniques, your spouse, children, grandchildren, and others for whom you care deeply will receive a far greater inheritance to enrich their lives. Therefore, even though you won't benefit personally after your death, you will live with the satisfaction of knowing that you have done all you could to pass on the fruits of your life's labor to your loved ones and causes that matter most to you.

Good estate planning settles not only the disposition of possessions and money but also other major life decisions, including custody of children. (If you have not appointed a guardian and a trustee for your minor children, when you die the state will appoint a guardian for your children. They may, or may not, be the persons you would have chosen to raise your children and oversee their assets.) We can't overemphasize this fact—if you die without a will or trust, a judge you never met will determine who's going to take care of your kids. For this reason alone, the small amount of time and money you invest now to dictate what happens when you die is well worth the effort. Planning your estate gives you the peace of mind of knowing that your affairs will be handled according to your wishes when you die.

Preparing for the Trip: What Estate Planning Entails

Estate planning is a process, not a product. It involves seeking advice, reviewing options, and creating a plan to ensure that

- ▶ your assets are sufficient to meet your objectives for your heirs
- ▶ your heirs receive those assets in the proportion, manner, and timeframe you choose
- ▶ income taxes, estate taxes, gift taxes, inheritance taxes, and transfer costs are minimized
- ▶ there is enough liquidity to pay taxes and transfer costs when they are due

Estate planning is not a one-shot deal. You need to review and update your estate plan at many different stages during your lifetime. Your plan will be affected by changes in your family, your wealth, your health, your charitable interests, and the laws and regulations that govern wealth transfer and taxation.

The consequences of not planning for your estate transfer can be severe. If your estate is illiquid (liquid assets are those where you can get the money or cash within a few days, for example, bank accounts; illiquid assets are the opposite: it could take months, even years to access that money, for example, your real estate) and you have not planned for estate tax payment, valuable assets may have to be sold to pay estate taxes. This could mean having to sell the family farm or business that you wanted to give, intact, to your children. It could mean having to sell securities or real estate when the market is down. It might even mean selling your surviving spouse's home. Estate tax, inheritance tax, and transfer costs can take more than 40 percent of your hard-earned estate away—before it goes to your heirs. Planning in advance can significantly increase the amount going to the people and charities you care about.

Other decisions you'll need to make as you design your plan include:

1. Who gets how much of your money and possessions (after the costs of settling the estate are subtracted).
2. How to give away many of your assets as tax-free gifts while you are still alive to minimize the assets socked by estate taxes when you die.
3. Who to name as a guardian for your children if they are younger than age 18.
4. Who to choose as trustee to administer any trusts you may establish.
5. Who to name as executor of your estate.
6. What you want done with your body after you die.
7. Who to appoint as successor custodian for the assets of a child or grandchild if you currently act as a custodian for a Uniform Gifts to Minors Act (UGMA) account.
8. What gifts of either money or property you wish to make to your favorite charity.
9. What advance directives you wish to make about health care you want provided or withheld in the event you cannot communicate your wishes. (You can also appoint someone you trust with a health care power of attorney.)

What to Pack

Examples of Property

Personal Property

- ▶ Cash and cash equivalents, including checking and savings accounts, money market accounts, savings bonds, and certificates of deposit
- ▶ Furniture of significant or sentimental value, such as antiques, fine furniture, and family heirlooms
- ▶ Other household items, such as large and small appliances, televisions, VCRs, CD players and stereos, electric tools, sterling silver, fine china, linens, crystal, etc.
- ▶ Artwork of significant value
- ▶ Clothing of significant value, such as furs and vintage clothing
- ▶ Collections of substantial value, such as stamp, doll, and coin collections
- ▶ Fine jewelry or jewelry with sentimental value
- ▶ Vehicles, including cars, boats, motorcycles, and motor homes

Investment Assets

- ▶ Stocks, bonds, and mutual funds
- ▶ Life insurance policies and other death benefits (including group)
- ▶ Retirement plans, such as pensions, annuities, IRAs, Keoghs, SEPs, and 401(k)s
- ▶ Business interests and business property

Real Property

- ▶ Residence
- ▶ Vacation home
- ▶ Direct ownership of other real estate

If you don't make these crucial decisions, they will be decided for you, often by people you don't know and in ways you may not approve. By taking care of these decisions in a calm, unhurried way, you avoid any need for a hastily drawn document or, even worse, a deathbed will, which might be contested later or, still worse, no will at all!

How Full Is Your Trunk? Determining What You Own

When you are ready to write your will, the first essential step is to create an inventory of your assets and your debts. Among other things, this information is essential when assessing the value of your estate, determining whether estate taxes are an issue for you, and helping you evaluate whether you should use other estate planning tools in addition to a will. Also, creating an inventory helps minimize the possibility that you will overlook some of your assets when you are creating your estate plan. Roadmap 1.1 will help you organize your asset and liability (debt) information and to estimate the total value of your estate. Once completed, your executor can use it to help ensure that all of your assets are accounted for.

Completing your asset inventory will probably be a relatively easy process for most of you. In fact, you may decide that you own so few assets that completing it is a waste of your time. That would be a mistake and could be dangerous. You may be surprised to discover just how much you own and the total value of your assets, especially if you are a homeowner.

It's time to begin the first step in the estate planning process—listing and categorizing your assets. If you're not sure what to include on your list, take a look at What to Pack (below) for examples of the kinds of property that should be included on your asset inventory worksheet (Roadmap 1.1 is the actual worksheet).

You will notice that the worksheet has spaces for listing and describing each of your assets, for indicating how you own each asset, for noting the percentage of each asset you own, and for recording each asset's estimated net value. Recording this information tells you several things:

▶ Which assets you can give away to your beneficiaries
▶ Which of your assets will go through probate
▶ Whether you should be concerned about minimizing the number of assets that will go through probate
▶ The total value of your assets and whether your estate will be subject to federal estate taxes

If your estate will be subject to taxes, minimizing those taxes should be one of your estate planning goals.

Describing Your Assets. To complete the asset inventory section of the estate worksheet, begin by clearly describing each of the assets you own, either as a 100 percent owner or as a partial or joint owner. List personal property of significant value, such as fine jewelry, furniture, and vehicles, as well as real property, which includes raw land, your home, and any other buildings

Estate Planning Worksheet

ASSET INVENTORY

Description of Asset	Type of Ownership	Percentage of Ownership	Net Value of Ownership
1. _____	_____	_____	_____
2. _____	_____	_____	_____
3. _____	_____	_____	_____
4. _____	_____	_____	_____
5. _____	_____	_____	_____
6. _____	_____	_____	_____
7. _____	_____	_____	_____

Total Current Value of Assets: $_____

LIABILITY INVENTORY

Description of Liability	Amount Owed (Your Share of Liability)
1. _____	_____
2. _____	_____
3. _____	_____
4. _____	_____
5. _____	_____
6. _____	_____
7. _____	_____

Total Current Liabilities: $_____

Total Assets: $_____

  (less)

Total Liabilities: $_____

  (plus)

Life Insurance Death Benefit: $_____

  (equals)

Total Value of Estate: $_____

you may own. Also, list any business interest you have as a sole proprietor, partner, or principal in a corporation.

Describe each of the assets you list on the worksheet using words that clearly identify the item. Your executor should not have to guess what you are referring to! Here are some suggestions for how to describe your property:

▶ *Checking and savings accounts and cash equivalents.* Note the type of account, the account number, and the name and address of the financial institution where the account is located.

▶ *Furniture.* For furniture of value, including antiques, family heirlooms, or collectible pieces, provide a short but precise description of each item. If a piece of furniture is associated with a particular era or style, such as a Chippendale chair or an art deco table, include that information.

▶ *Other household items.* You may want to group certain items with relatively low value together rather than listing each item individually. For example, "All the cooking and kitchen supplies at (your address)" or "All the hand tools and electric tools at (your address)."

▶ *Artwork.* Describe the subject as well as the artist and the particular era or style of any significant paintings, sculptures, or other artwork you may own. Miscellaneous, less important artwork can be identified with a single description, such as "All the paintings and other artwork at (your address)."

▶ *Clothing.* List furs, expensive designer clothes, or significant items of vintage clothing separately. Describe them in as much detail as possible, including, when applicable, the name of the designer and the particular style and/or date. Less valuable clothing can be grouped together such as "All the items of female (or male) clothing at (your address)."

▶ *Collections.* If you own a significant collection of stamps, coins, books, dolls, antique pens or autographs, salt and pepper shakers, and so on, describe it briefly. Include the number of items in the collection and the era of those items when applicable; for example, "salt and pepper shakers from the 1920s and 1930s" or "antique china dolls from the nineteenth century."

▶ *Jewelry.* List each piece of fine jewelry. Do the same for any family heirlooms. Specify what the item is made of—gold, silver, types of stones—and the style and era of the piece. If you own a collection of good quality, collectible costume jewelry, you may want to list it as a single item—"All the costume jewelry at (your address)." However, if any of the items can be considered antiques of value, list them separately.

► *Vehicles.* List each vehicle separately. Note its color, make and model, manufacturer, year of manufacture, license number, and Vehicle Identification Number (VIN).

► *Stocks and mutual funds.* For each investment, include the name of the company or name of the fund, number of shares you own, relevant CU-SIP number, relevant account number, and the name of the brokerage company where the account is held.

► *Bonds.* Note the name of the relevant company or government entity, cost of each bond purchased, and the date purchased.

► *Life insurance policies.* For each policy, indicate the policy number, the name of the company that issued the policy, and the name of the policy beneficiary or beneficiaries.

► *Retirement plans.* Note the type of plan, the applicable account number if any, and the company that is administering the plan.

► *Business interests.* If you own an interest in a business, specify the type of business—partnership, corporation, sole proprietorship—and note your share of the business. (If your business is a sole proprietorship, you own 100 percent of it.) If you have an interest in a corporation, indicate the number of shares you own; also, indicate the name and location of the business.

► *Land and buildings, including your home.* List the complete address of each piece of property you own. If you own a second home, such as a lake or ski house, and you intend to leave both the home and its furnishings to a beneficiary, include the home's furnishings in your description of the property—for example, "Vacation home and all furnishings located at (address of your vacation home)." If you own raw land without a specific address, indicate the number of acres you own and their approximate location, including the nearest town or city and the county where the acreage is located.

Type of Ownership. Indicate how you own each of the assets on your worksheet so that you know what you can and cannot give away. You may own 100 percent of an asset or you may own an asset as a joint tenant with right of survivorship, as a tenant by the entirety, or as a tenant in common (see Chapter 3). In addition, the assets you own are either separate or community property. To save time and space when completing this section of the work-sheet, you may want to abbreviate each type of ownership. For example:

► J.T.W.R.O.S.—joint tenant with right of survivorship
► T.E.—tenant by the entirety
► T.C.—tenant in common
► C.P.—community property
► S.P.— separate property

Note: You cannot use your will to transfer assets like life insurance policy benefits, the benefits from an employee retirement plan, or the funds in an IRA or Keogh because you designated the beneficiaries for those assets when you set them up. Therefore, use the abbreviation D.B. (designated beneficiary) in the Type of Ownership column when you record one of these assets on your worksheet.

Percentage of Ownership. In the column titled Percentage of Ownership indicate the percentage of each asset that you own. For example, if you own an asset by yourself, that figure will be 100 percent. The percentage will be smaller if you own the asset with one or more persons.

Net Value of Ownership. In the worksheet's final column, record the current market value of each asset you have listed. In most instances, current market value is what you could sell the asset for today, not what you bought it for. However, in the case of a bank account, current market value is simply the amount of money in the account.

You should be able to determine the market value of an employee benefit plan, IRA, Keogh, brokerage account, or the like by referring to your most current account statement or by calling the plan administrator or the company with whom you maintain each investment. If you monitor your investments online, you can also determine their market values by going to the Web site where you maintain your investment information.

If you are unsure of the value of any antiques, artwork, or collectibles you may own, consider having them professionally appraised, especially if you feel that the asset's value is significant. An appraisal helps guard against over- or undervaluing an asset and helps make sure you are appropriately insured. The appraiser you use should have specific experience appraising the particular type of asset you want valued.

If you own a business or have an interest in one, you may want to consult an experienced certified public accountant to determine the value of your share. As an overview, however, if your business is a sole proprietorship, its value is the dollar amount you could sell the business for. If you're in a partnership or a limited liability corporation, the value of your share could be how much you would be compensated by the business if you were to retire from it or your share of the business's liquidation value. If you have an interest in a closely held corporation, the value of your share of the business and of any buyout agreements that may be in effect need to be considered. If the corporation is publicly held, the value of your business interest depends on the number of shares of the business you own and its current stock price.

Don't worry if some of your asset valuations are approximations. Unless you pull numbers out of thin air, reasonable approximate valuations should not create problems.

Determining What You Owe. Your liabilities may include outstanding bank or personal loans you're obligated to pay, credit card debt, property liens, debts to the IRS and other taxing entities, outstanding court judgments rendered against you, and any past-due child support or alimony you may be obligated to pay. (Don't worry about including periodic small obligations like your monthly utility and phone bills.)

Your liabilities may also include your share of any outstanding debts related to an asset you may own with others. Let's assume, for example, you own a beach house with two friends as joint tenants and the market value of the house is $90,000. If the balance on the beach house mortgage is $30,000 and you and your co-owners also owe $5,000 in back taxes, your share of the total debt (liability) associated with that asset is $11,667 because you have a one-third interest in the property.

When you complete the liability section of your worksheet, be sure to include the total amount you owe for each debt and relevant account numbers as well as the names and addresses of the companies, government agencies, or individuals to whom you owe the money.

Estimated Net Value of Your Estate. To determine the estimated net value of your estate, add together the values of all the assets listed on your worksheet and then subtract from that number the total value of the liabilities. If you are determining the net value of your estate in 2006, you do not need to worry about federal estate taxes if its value is less than $2,000,000.

YEAR OF DEATH	FILING REQUIREMENT
2005, 2006, 2007	$2,000,000
2009	$3,500,000

Source: Internal Revenue Service (http://www.irs.gov/publications/p950/)

Although state estate and inheritance taxes may be a concern for some of you, note that the threshold increases stop in 2009, at which time only estates worth more than $3.5 million will be liable for federal estate taxes. The estate tax is repealed for 2010 and reinstated in 2011. If estate taxes are a concern for you, be sure to consult with a qualified financial planner or an estate planning attorney about what you can do to reduce the size of your taxable estate.

Review and update your estate planning worksheet on a regular basis. During your lifetime, you will probably gain and also lose or sell assets. Furthermore, the value of your assets is likely to appreciate or depreciate, and you may take on new debt or pay off existing debt. Your estate planning worksheet should reflect each change because a change may affect your net worth as well as the kind of estate planning you should do.

▶ Avoid Surprises: Prepare for Roadblocks

Sometimes saying nothing says a lot to others. The problem is that it probably doesn't say what you really mean. By failing to plan your estate, you cannot come back at a later date and tell your family and friends that you really did care. Failing to plan leaves the message that you really didn't care enough. You put thought into what you are going to wear each day, where to have lunch, what you will do over the weekend. Why not put some thought into what will happen if you do not have a tomorrow to fix things? Most people put more time and effort into planning their summer vacation than they do into how they are going to take care of their families after they die. Is that the message you want to pass on to your family—that a vacation was worth more of your attention than planning for them in their time of need?

The purpose of your estate plan is to ensure that you can pass on the messages you want, to the people you care about, under the conditions that you dictate.

Dear Attorney Marks,

I was 22 when we got married. Bruce was 28 and had been married once before and had a three-year-old daughter. When our son was born two years later, I started asking Bruce about doing a will. He thought I was being silly. We were young, why did we need a will? He was a good father and a good husband; I couldn't understand why he was so stubborn about this.

When Bruce's boss called and said there was an accident at the construction site, and Bruce was being flown to the nearest trauma hospital, I raced to the hospital, but by the time I got there, Bruce had died. Before I even had time to make the funeral arrangements, Bruce's ex-wife called, asking what provisions Bruce had made for Brianna. I told her that Bruce had not made any arrangements, but she thinks I'm lying and is threatening to sue me. We have a nice home and some money in the bank, and a $50,000 life insurance policy, but that will just barely help us pay off the mortgage and the burial expenses. I love Brianna and would gladly make sure she is provided for, but I also needed to provide for our son and me.

How can I prove that there is no will, no trust, nothing indicating how Bruce wanted his estate to be divided? I'm desperate; can you help us?

Janine

Even if you are not married, do not have children, are not a millionaire, and have all of your assets in retirement accounts with designated beneficiaries, you should consider preparing an estate plan. Like Bruce, you may have few assets (or all your assets in designated retirement accounts), but if you have minor children, you need to provide guardianship, and it is likely some assets like vehicles, collectibles, and employer-provided life insurance may not have designated beneficiaries. Even if you have no children, you still have assets to pass on to other heirs or charitable causes.

Essential Travel Documents: Estate Planning Basics

Will. Your family structure also plays an important role in the need for a will. Almost all single or married people need a will. However, it is even more important for anyone who has remarried to consider preparing a will (or revising an existing one), especially if either spouse has children from a prior relationship.

That's because intestate (the term used to refer to dying without a will) laws dictate disposition of assets and guardianships for minor children.

A common myth is that someone who is unmarried and has no children doesn't need a will, but a will also ensures the ultimate disposition of financial assets, even personal mementos. Every state has a generic will for residents who die intestate. It's written for the masses, and you may not like the choices that would be carried out on your behalf.

Revocable Living Trust (Inter Vivos Trust). This is a document that functions much like a will. You contribute some, or all, of your assets to the trust while you are alive. Because it's revocable, you may change its provisions or even revoke the trust anytime, for any reason, during your life. The two main benefits are the avoidance of the probate process and costs and to provide instructions to others during a period of incapacity (as opposed to only after death, as with a will). While it is a very useful estate tool, it is not needed for all individuals. You should learn more about the benefits of a trust and the costs of establishing one, then determine if it's right for you.

What to Pack tells you about the primary documents that you would want to look at when planning your estate.

Other Significant Documents. Even if you have a will, that's not enough to be prepared properly. You also need a series of ancillary documents that address incapacity and other issues short of death. These include a financial power of attorney and medical care documents.

Power of attorney. Financial power of attorney, or durable power of attorney for finance, provides for the appointment of someone to make financial decisions for you. This power may go into effect immediately on signing the document, or it may be delayed until an event occurs that triggers the power or until you are unable to manage your own financial affairs. This delayed

What to Pack

The Primary Documents

- ▶ Will
- ▶ Revocable Living Trust
- ▶ Power of attorney
- ▶ Medical documents
- ▶ Living Will
- ▶ Durable Power of Attorney for Healthcare
- ▶ Funeral directive

activation is known as a springing power. The power of attorney can include specific provisions allowing for financial activities that may otherwise cease if you become incapacitated. Having this document eliminates the need for your family to petition the court to appoint a financial guardian or conservator. As with all financial and legal decisions affecting your life, it is important to consider carefully to whom you give this power. Once in force, the individual with the power of attorney will be able to represent you in your financial affairs at any time. You should also consult with an attorney for rules that may be specific to your state of residence or domicile.

Medical documents. Medical care documents generally include the following:

- ▶ A directive to physicians, sometimes known as a living will, tells medical personnel what, if any, means of artificial life support you would want and under what circumstances, in the event of your medical incapacity.
- ▶ Durable Power of Attorney for Healthcare names someone to make medical decisions on your behalf if you can't.

In addition you may wish to prepare a funeral directive; that is, written instructions telling your family whether you want to be buried or cremated and whether you want to donate your organs. You may also want to include information about your funeral or memorial service, and, if you have purchased a burial plot and arranged for a casket, you should include that information as well.

You can save much headache—and additional needless heartache—by doing your basic estate planning now.

▶ Traveling Companions: Professional Help or Do-It-Yourself?

Keep in mind that estate planning, tax planning, and asset protection often go hand in hand. In most cases, the three areas complement each other. In some cases, there will be a trade-off between tax advantages, estate planning, and asset protection. Therefore, we generally recommend that you contact your estate planning attorney and/or tax advisor before proceeding. In some cases, you may also want to involve a financial planner, and your accountant.

However, if you have few assets and a limited number of people or causes to whom you want those assets distributed, the process does not have to be complicated or expensive (a common excuse people use for not planning their estate). Several do-it-yourself books on the market can help you draw up a simple will and prepare other documents that will be useful in various life situations. If you own a computer, several easy-to-use computer programs —such as Nolo's Living Trust Maker, Quicken Family Lawyer, and Quicken WillMaker—ask you a series of questions, and then format your answers into legal documents that protect you and your estate against almost every eventuality. (See Appendix B for more information.) You can also obtain a standard will that you could customize to meet your circumstances from a legal clinic or local law firm.

On the other hand, if you hold substantial assets, or your wishes for giving away assets are complicated, you should consider assembling a team of financial experts to make sure that your estate plan covers every contingency. And because estate and probate laws vary from state to state, it is important to have your documents drawn in accordance with local laws by an attorney familiar with them.

Before You Start, Get Directions

If you have a sizeable estate or anything but the simplest of wishes, when you do your own estate plan without seeking advice from authoritative sources, you are potentially jeopardizing those you love by leaving them with un- necessary problems. There are good reasons why we have lawyers, who are trained to do things like drafting wills and trusts. That is not to say that all lawyers are competent in areas such as estate planning, but they are much more likely to know how to get where you want to go or direct you to someone who can. Without getting professional help, you can easily be setting up your family to get lost in a foreign land, or, at the very least, to take some long, unnecessary detours.

As anyone who has traveled knows, when you are in unfamiliar territory and don't speak the language, you do not always know where the problem areas may be or how to avoid them. You need to rely on competent guides to get you to your intended destination. As travelers also know, some guides are better than others, and not all lawyers are competent professionals in the area of estate planning.

Choosing the Right Driver: Selecting a Lawyer

You need to choose a lawyer who is competent. You should feel confident that your lawyer will draft your estate plan to best reflect your intentions. Here are five characteristics you should look for in an estate planning attorney:

1. *Good educational background.* Not all attorneys are educated alike. An attorney from a well-established law school is more likely to provide valuable insight as well as sound drafting skills than someone from a weaker law school. Attorneys with LL.M. degrees in taxation or estate planning are more likely to have stronger skills than attorneys who stopped their education after receiving their law degree. An LL.M. is a master of laws, which means that the attorney has taken an extra year of courses in a specialized area.

2. *Experience.* Estate planning is not a black-and-white area of the law. It takes some time and experience to understand a client's needs. Any lawyer can draft a will, but it takes some time to learn how to draft a will that properly reflects a person's intentions. There is no rule of thumb on how long it takes a lawyer to learn these skills, but it is probably safe to say that there needs to be at least a couple of years of full-time work in this area before an attorney can become skilled enough to know the right questions to ask clients. It is also helpful for a lawyer to see an estate plan through to its fruition. How do you know the drafted documents are any good if the lawyer hasn't had any clients who have died?

3. *Specialization in estate planning law.* An attorney who practices medical malpractice law, criminal defense law, and estate planning is not spend-

Dear Susan Smith, Esq.

My parents were kind but unsophisticated. As they started getting older, my brother and I suggested they write a will. Finally, they agreed to go to a lawyer, although Dad didn't want to spend the money. They didn't show us the wills, and we didn't ask to see them.

Dad, Mom, and Terry died in an accident together. I met with the attorney who drew up the wills. He told me that Mom's cousin Jennifer got 25 percent of the estate, and that Terry and I split the rest, but since Terry was dead, Terry's wife would receive Terry's portion. Terry and his wife had been living apart, and, although not legally separated, there were hard feelings between them. My parents would never put such a provision in their wills! When I asked, the lawyer said it was a standard provision—a deceased child's spouse inherits the deceased child's share of the estate. I'm certain he could not have discussed this with them.

Worse still, the wills didn't say that cousin Jennifer got 25 percent and Terry and I split the rest. It said that she got 25 percent, Terry got the shop, and I got the rest. As written, Jennifer's share comes from my portion of the estate, not Terry's. My parents wanted to make sure that Terry got the shop, since he worked there, and the lawyer says this was the only way to do that, although they didn't specifically discuss it. My parents couldn't have understood that this meant I would inherit only about 25 percent of the estate. Is there anything I can do?

John Johnson

ing enough time in the area of estate planning to excel in the field. You should always ask how much of an attorney's time is devoted to estate planning. Another way to ask the question is to ask how many wills and trusts the attorney drafts per month. If the answer is less than five, it is probably safe to assume that estate planning is not their sole means of support.

4. *Additional credentials beyond the law degree.* Look for an LL.M. degree, a certified specialist designation (many states allow attorneys to hold themselves out as specialists only after the person has demonstrated extreme competency in their field), or membership in ACTEC (American College of Trust and Estates Counsel). ACTEC members must have been practicing law for 10 or more years and be recognized for their contributions to estate planning through writing and speaking endeavors.

5. *Trustworthiness.* Does your intuition tell you your estate planning attorney is someone who will be there when your spouse or other family members die? This is someone with whom you will need to share your intimate family secrets, if you are going to develop a plan that is tailored to your family. You want someone who can be trusted and with whom you, your spouse, your children, and your other loved ones feel comfortable.

After you have chosen a lawyer, make sure you read and understand the documents that are prepared for you. There will always be some legal jargon that is hard to get through, but you need to understand whether or not your intentions are reflected in the documents. Your attorney should prepare a summary letter that is in English, not legalese, describing your estate planning documents. If your attorney does not prepare such a letter as a matter of practice, you should ask for one. Without a succinct summary, how will you know whether the documents properly reflect your intentions? It is not your estate plan until it says what you want it to say.

Learn the Language

Key Terms to Know When Designing Your Itinerary

beneficiary the person, charitable organization, pet, and so on you choose to leave your money and/or other assets to in your will, in a trust, a custodial account, or the like.

bequest a gift made under or through a will.

estate everything that you own at the time of your death.

estate planning a multifaceted process that involves planning for the disposal of your assets after you die. It may also include taking steps to minimize the amount of estate taxes your estate must pay and to speed up the transfer of your assets to your beneficiaries. Estate planning also includes writing a living will and giving someone a durable power of attorney for health care.

executor person you name in your will to help settle your estate by taking it through the probate process after your death. Your choice for executor must be officially appointed by the court.

guardian (conservator) in law, the person you name in your will to raise your minor child should you and the child's other parent both die.

heir a relative who is legally entitled, according to your state's laws, to inherit from your estate if you die without a will.

inheritance tax a tax paid by the beneficiary of an estate in some states.

inter vivos gift a gift that you make to a beneficiary while you are alive.

intestate dying without a legally valid will.

living trust (inter vivos trust) a trust that you set up while you are alive; can be irrevocable or revocable, although most living trusts are revocable.

living will a health care directive that spells out your wishes regarding the specific types of end-of-life care and treatment you do and do not want.

minor child in law, a child who is younger than 18 or 21 depending on the state.

personal property everything you own other than real property, which includes your home, other buildings, and land.

power of attorney a legal document that gives someone the right to act on your behalf; may give someone else the right to make financial and/or health and medical care decisions for you; may be temporary or it can last until you take it away (durable power of attorney).

probate legal process that proves the validity of your will, officially appoints your executor, pays your estate taxes, if any are due, and any legitimate creditor claims against your estate, and distributes the property in your estate to your beneficiaries according to the terms of your will.

real property real estate that includes homes and other buildings as well as land.

taxable estate the assets in your estate that are subject to federal and state estate taxes after your death.

tenants in common a type of joint property ownership that gives each owner a share of an asset without an interest in the shares of the other owner(s) or the right of survivorship. Each owner can sell or give away their share without the consent of the other owners.

trust a legal entity that you can create to own and manage assets for the benefit of one or more beneficiaries.

trustee the person who is named in the trust document to manage trust assets.

Uniform Gifts to Minors Act or Uniform Transfers to Minors Act federal laws that permit you to establish a custodial account for a minor child and to place certain types of assets in the account.

will a legal document that spells out what you want to happen to your assets after you die; may also designate both a personal and a property guardian for a minor child.

Map Your Trip

Planning, Writing, and Executing a Will

▶ Giving Directions: Your Will

Whether you do it yourself or with the help of financial advisors, writing a will is key to estate planning. A will is, quite simply, a legal declaration that gives instructions on how to dispose of your assets when you die. You can divide your assets any way you want, as long as guidelines are presented clearly in writing. (Some states prohibit clauses in wills that are considered illegal, bizarre, or against public policy.)

When you write your will, you have a minimum of three critical decisions to make:

▶ Who to name as executor of your estate
▶ To whom to leave your property; that is, who your beneficiaries will be
▶ What to give to each of your beneficiaries

If you have a minor child or children, you will also have to decide who to name as their guardian. As we travel down this road, we show you how to make certain that the decisions you make will be properly carried out.

Planning Your Itinerary: The Basics of Writing and Executing a Will

As we saw in Chapter 1, your will includes both tangible assets, like homes, cars, boats, artwork, collectibles, and furniture, as well as intangible assets, like bank accounts, stocks, bonds, and mutual funds. To specify that certain people should inherit particular tangible assets, insert in your will a provision known as a Tangible Personal Property Memorandum (TPPM).

Other rights and benefits, like pension rights and life insurance proceeds, are normally handled outside of your will. For example, life insurance proceeds are usually payable directly to the beneficiaries. And property owned jointly with rights of survivorship, such as a home held with your spouse, is not affected by the will because, by law, when you die it passes to that joint owner automatically.

Also, any property that you have placed in a trust passes to the beneficiary without going through your will or probate. Because trusts take assets out of your probate estate, they can save you a lot of money.

Usually, you will create what is known as a simple will, which provides for the outright distribution of assets to the beneficiaries. If your will establishes trusts to receive assets, it is a testamentary trust will. If you set up trusts before your death and the will passes assets into those trusts, it is a pour-over will.

Husbands and wives can write their wills either jointly or separately. Most estate lawyers suggest separate wills because it is difficult to establish who owns which property in a joint will. In addition, after one spouse dies, it is troublesome for the surviving spouse to change the provisions in a joint will. And if you're not careful, a joint will might deprive you of the full lifetime tax-exempt inheritance that both husband and wife are allowed to pass on to heirs free of federal estate tax.

Another important aspect of your will is choosing an executor of your estate.

This can be either a qualified family member, a long-time, trusted friend with knowledge of financial affairs, or an institution, like a bank or law firm, with financial and legal expertise. The executor's task is to carry out your wishes as set forth in the will as efficiently as possible. This process may take several months, or it may drag on for years. If you trust the executor completely, give the executor enough authority to take action so that the person does not have to buy a surety bond (sometimes called a fidelity bond), which insures your estate against malfeasance by the executor. The cost of that bond, which can be substantial, is paid by your estate.

When you visit a lawyer about your will, be well prepared. Bring with you the following information:

1. A list of your real property, such as homes, and your tangible personal property, such as cars and furniture. Indicate how much you paid for each and what you estimate its present worth to be; also indicate where the property is located and whether you own it solely or jointly.

2. A list of intangible property, such as bank accounts, stocks, bonds, and mutual funds. Bring your latest bank and brokerage statements.

3. A list of all insurance policies and all pension and other employee benefits. Bring your latest statements.

4. A list of all your debts, including debts to banks, insurance companies, your employer, the IRS, and individuals. Bring any documents outlining your liabilities. Note: If you completed Roadmap 1.1 you already have this information.

5. The names, addresses, and telephone numbers of any professional you want contacted, such as your financial advisor, CPA, banker, or another lawyer. Also bring the names, addresses, and phone numbers of the executor and any guardians named for your children. Include, of course, the names, addresses, and telephone numbers of your spouse and children.

Once the will has been completed, review it every five years or so to keep it up-to-date. If new circumstances have developed, change the will accordingly (see below).

Do not have someone who is a potential beneficiary of the will witness your signature. Employees in your lawyer's office normally act as witnesses. All the witnesses should sign the will in the presence of each other and should note their addresses so they can be contacted later, if necessary. With these signatures, your will is self-proved, allowing your executor to avoid the complex process of proving the authenticity of your will in probate court. Your will becomes effective only after you die and a probate court accepts the will as legally valid.

Once your will is complete, keep the signed original and several unsigned copies. (If all the copies are signed, no one will know which the actual, fully executed will is.) Preserve the original in a secure place other than a safe-deposit box, which may be sealed at your death, making it very difficult for the executor to administer your will. Keep copies in several locations such as in a file cabinet at home, with your banker or lawyer, and with the executor of your estate. Your executor likely should hold a signed, fully executable copy. You can even file a copy with the probate registrar at your county courthouse for a small fee.

If you leave nothing to someone who expects to be included in your will —especially a relative—expect your heirs to face a battle. People will fight like cats and dogs over property if they feel they have been slighted. They often contest the will on some technicality, claiming the document was not properly executed. For example, they might propose that someone with evil intent unduly influenced you while you drafted the will. Or they might say you had no mental capacity to make decisions when you excluded them from the will. Or they might even try to prove that the will was altered fraudulently and should therefore be overruled. In any case, when someone contests your will for whatever reason, it can create enmity among your heirs for years and prevent your beneficiaries from receiving expeditiously what you wanted them to have. For this reason, many lawyers suggest acknowledging these potential heirs in your will. This makes it obvious that you did not forget them; e.g., "to my estranged sister Stephanie I leave nothing of my estate."

▶ Accident Insurance: Living Will and Health Care Power of Attorney

If you become fatally ill or injured and can't make your own decisions or let your doctors know what kinds of life-prolonging medical care and treatment you do or don't want, you should make this known much before the unfortunate event actually occurs. Modern medicine and medical technology can keep you alive, sometimes indefinitely, whether the care and treatment you receive reflect your wishes or not. The cost of that care and treatment can deplete your estate; therefore, planning for this possibility should be part of your estate planning.

Anyone who has ever been in the hospital or had a relative or close friend hospitalized knows just how quickly the medical bills can add up. Even with good health insurance, a serious illness or accident can eat up your savings and maybe even force you to liquidate valuable assets, thus diminishing the size of your estate. This is especially true if you are critically ill or injured and life-sustaining measures are used to keep you alive as long as possible.

An increasing number of people are dealing with this possibility by preparing health care directives, including a living will and a durable power of attorney for health care. You can use these documents to control the kinds of health care and treatment you will receive if you are terminally ill or critically injured and can't speak for yourself. You may want to prepare health care directives for the following reasons:

▶ You don't want to be kept alive at all costs when there is no reasonable hope of recovery.

▶ You don't want your loved ones to go through the emotional pain of watching you die little by little.

▶ You don't want to put your loved ones in the position of guessing about the kinds of health care and treatment you would or would not want if you could speak for yourself. You especially don't want them to have to decide whether to end the care and treatment that is keeping you alive.

▶ You want to spare your loved ones the time and expense involved in petitioning the court to have a conservator appointed to handle your affairs.

▶ You don't want to see the assets in your estate depleted by costly medical care and treatment when there is no reasonable hope of recovery.

If You're Hurt En Route: Protection if You Are Incapacitated

It is also possible that you may become physically or mentally incapacitated for a limited period and unable to manage your own affairs. Estate planning also includes planning for how decisions related to your business and personal affairs will be made under such circumstances. This type of planning is especially important if you are a business owner and your family depends on the business for its livelihood. Without such planning, your business could be financially damaged or ruined and your family's finances devastated. We will discuss health care directives below (if you own a business be sure to look at Chapter 6 where your business and your estate are addressed in greater detail).

Living Will. A living will is a written document that speaks for you if you are too ill or too injured to speak for yourself, and is activated when you become mentally or physically incapacitated and have no realistic hope of returning to your normal life. While a traditional will distributes your assets upon your death, a living will must be enforced while you live. It states whether or not you wish to be kept alive by extraordinary artificial life-support systems and authorizes doctors and named relatives or trusted friends to disconnect any equipment keeping you alive. It lets your loved ones and physicians know your wishes regarding the use of various life-sustaining treatments and equipment, including respirators, breathing tubes, cardiac assist pumps, intravenous tubes, artificial nutrition tubes, artificial hydration, dialysis, cardiopulmonary resuscitation, and so on. It can spell out what you do want as well as what you don't want. You can use it to provide your doctors with "do not resuscitate" instructions, "do all you can" instructions, or something in between.

Most states now recognize your right to die. Courts usually side with patients who have given explicit instructions in advance that they do not want their lives extended artificially. Valid living wills usually do not expire unless they are revoked. However, it's a good idea to review the document every year or so. Initial and date it at each review to make sure readers know that it still reflects your wishes.

Preparing a Living Will. The easiest way to execute what is called an advance directive, which includes a living will and medical power of attorney, is to use one of the standardized forms available from most estate-planning lawyers. You can write your own living will without the help of an attorney by using a living will fill-in-the-blanks form, available from a local hospital, bar association, or government agency on aging. Also, several national nonprofit organizations offer living wills specific to each state. Among them are

▶ Partnership for Caring: 1620 Eye Street NW, Suite 202, Washington, DC 20006; Telephone: 202-296-8071; 800-989-9455. You can download its form at the organization's Web site at http://www.partnershipforcaring. org/Advance. If you don't order online, there is a small fee for the form.

▶ Aging with Dignity: P.O. Box 1661, Tallahassee, FL, 32302-1661; Telephone: 850-681-2010; http://www.agingwithdignity.org. Its "Five Wishes" living will is much more detailed than the one available through Partnership for Caring, but it may not be legally valid in every state. For more information about the Five Wishes living will, or to order a copy of the document, call or go to the organization's Web site. The cost of the living will is $5 plus handling and shipping charges.

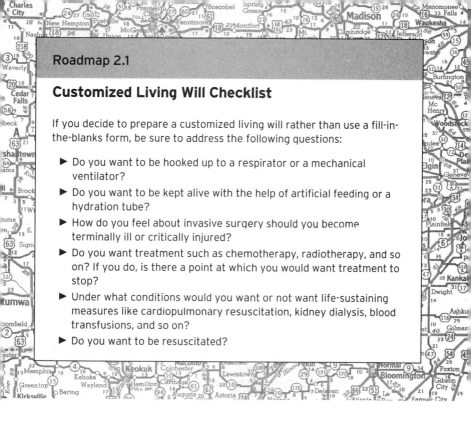

Roadmap 2.1

Customized Living Will Checklist

If you decide to prepare a customized living will rather than use a fill-in-the-blanks form, be sure to address the following questions:

▶ Do you want to be hooked up to a respirator or a mechanical ventilator?

▶ Do you want to be kept alive with the help of artificial feeding or a hydration tube?

▶ How do you feel about invasive surgery should you become terminally ill or critically injured?

▶ Do you want treatment such as chemotherapy, radiotherapy, and so on? If you do, is there a point at which you would want treatment to stop?

▶ Under what conditions would you want or not want life-sustaining measures like cardiopulmonary resuscitation, kidney dialysis, blood transfusions, and so on?

▶ Do you want to be resuscitated?

Using a standard fill-in-the-blanks form is okay as long as it adheres to the laws of your state. If the form does not allow you to adequately address all of your concerns and preferences, prepare your own living will with the help of an attorney. Roadmap 2.1 reviews the issues that should be addressed in that living will.

Sign your living will in front of two impartial adults who are not related to you, who stand to inherit nothing from you, and who are not doctors or hospital employees who might be in a position to disconnect your life-support equipment. In conjunction with the living will, sign a health care power of attorney form, which gives someone you trust the power to make medical decisions for you if you are unable to do so.

Store your living will in a fireproof safe at home or in a safe-deposit box along with other important medical records. Make sure someone besides you knows the combination to the safe or has a key to the safe-deposit box.

Also, give a copy of your living will to your spouse, your unmarried partner, a close family member, a good friend, and the executor of your estate. Review the document with whoever has a copy of your living will so that you can provide explanations of your wishes as necessary and the person will feel comfortable if your living will has to be activated.

In most states, you must let your doctor know that you have a living will. Even if that is not a requirement in your state, reviewing your living will with your doctor is an excellent idea. That way you can be sure that your doctor feels comfortable with the wishes you have stated in it. If your doctor does not feel comfortable, you can find a doctor who will enforce it. Ask your doctor to keep a copy of your living will with your medical records.

Legal Requirements for Living Wills. Living wills are recognized in all states. However, every state has its own criteria for what makes a living will legally valid and enforceable. Your living will must have certain characteristics to be legally valid.

1. You must be a legal adult when you write or execute your living will. Depending on your state, the age of legal adulthood is either 18 or 21.
2. You must be mentally competent at the time you write or execute your living will.
3. Your living will must be written; no state recognizes an oral living will.
4. Two adults must sign, date, and witness your living will. In most states, neither of the adults can be your legal heirs.
5. Your living will must be notarized.

Changing or Revoking a Living Will. You can change or revoke your living will whenever you want. However, be sure you do it according to your state's rules for amendments and revocations.

In most states, all you need to do to revoke a living will is write on the document that it's no longer valid. If anyone has a copy of the living will you are invalidating, be sure to get those copies back. Do the same if you registered your living will with your state. Some states require registration.

Activating a Living Will. Generally, your living will cannot be activated until you are near death and two doctors (sometimes one) have stated in writing that you're unable to make your own decisions and are terminally ill or permanently unconscious. If you are in a great deal of pain but conscious and death is not imminent, your living will won't go into effect.

Normally, if your doctors are aware that you have a living will and if the document is legally valid, they are expected to comply with it. However, occasionally doctors ignore the directives of your living will or delay processing the paperwork required to activate it. Doctors do this for several reasons:

1. They are uncomfortable with the provisions in your living will.
2. Your family does not want your living will to be activated and pressures your doctors to ignore it.
3. Your doctors disagree about your condition or your medical prognosis.
4. The provisions of your will are too vague to be enforced.

To minimize the chance that your family will interfere with the activation of your living will, you should ask them to read it, explain your requests, and answer any questions they may have. If your loved ones understand your thinking, they are more apt to respect your wishes.

If you are terminally ill or critically injured and your doctors will not comply with the directives in your living will, your family can ask that you be transferred to a more sympathetic physician. However, switching at this point can be difficult. Therefore, your family may need to consult with an attorney who specializes in elder care law and ultimately the matter might have to be decided in court.

If You Don't Have a Living Will. If you become critically ill and you don't have a living will, the doctor in charge of your care will decide what treatment you will receive. Although your doctor may consult with your spouse and other close family members, in the absence of a living will the doctor is not obligated to comply with your family's wishes.

If your family wants to stop certain kinds of medical care and treatment because it believes you wouldn't want it and your doctor is not willing to comply, a court hearing may be held to resolve the stalemate. That hearing will involve legal costs for your family, it can be time consuming, and may also be emotionally draining for them. Another option for your family is to find a new doctor more sympathetic to its wishes, which may again require involvement of the court. A third option is for your family to petition the court to have a conservator appointed who will make medical decisions for you.

Conservators. If your family petitions the court for the appointment of a conservator to make health care decisions for you, a hearing will be held to establish that you are not mentally competent to make these decisions for yourself. If the court agrees with your family, it will appoint a conservator, possibly a family member. This person may have to get the court's approval before being able to make certain decisions, and involving the court slows things down.

Durable Power of Attorney for Health Care. Giving someone a durable power of attorney for health care is one of the best ways to ensure that your living will is enforced. The person who has the power of attorney can speak for you regarding your health care and treatment, and push to have your living will activated if your family or doctor is reluctant to. This person can also make medical and health decisions on your behalf when you are dying.

If you are in a committed but unmarried relationship, and especially if you are in a same-sex relationship, in many states, your doctor may not consult with your partner about what to do. The best way to ensure that your partner is consulted is to give them a durable power of attorney for your health care. (Your partner should also have a copy of your living will.)

In some states, the person to whom you give a durable power of attorney for health care can make these same decisions when you are physically or mentally incapacitated but when death is not an immediate threat. Therefore, a durable power of attorney for health care is a more comprehensive and powerful legal tool than a living will.

The person to whom you give this power must be a legal adult and, obviously, should be someone you trust completely. The person must have the personal strength to make potentially difficult decisions on your behalf, and must be willing to accept this important responsibility.

Check with your state attorney general's office or with the medical board in your state or county to find out whether there are any legal restrictions on the person to whom you can grant a durable power of attorney for health care.

The best kind of durable power of attorney for health care is one that not only specifies the kinds of medical care and treatment you do and don't want but also spells out your values and personal beliefs about such things as life-sustaining measures, pain, the relative cost of various procedures and treatments, and other quality-of-life issues. You may also want to describe what you consider to be an acceptable quality of life. In your instructions, be as clear and specific as possible so that nothing is left to interpretation. Furthermore, don't just write down this information; discuss it with that individual.

You can use a fill-in-the-blanks form as long as it meets your state's requirements. You can obtain it from the same organizations that provide living wills. You can also hire an attorney to prepare a durable power of attorney for health care that reflects your particular needs and concerns.

Changing or Revoking a Durable Power of Attorney for Health Care. You can change or revoke a durable power of attorney for health care whenever you wish, as long as you are mentally competent. If you change it, make sure you adhere to the laws of your state. If you revoke it, prepare a formal notice of revocation. Also, if you gave copies of your durable power of attorney for health care to other people, get them back and destroy them, then provide these people with a new set of valid health care directives.

Organ Donation. The Uniform Anatomical Gift Act allows you to indicate whether you want your organs to be donated to others after your death. Donating an organ so that someone else may live is perhaps the greatest gift you can give to anyone.

As a part of your planning, obtain an organ donor card from your state's department of motor vehicles. Complete the card and have it witnessed. Keep it in your wallet, date book, checkbook, or anything else you always carry with you. In some states, you can become an organ donor when you get or renew your driver's license. Your donation wishes are printed on the back of your license.

Make sure that your doctor, close family members, and the person with the durable power of attorney for your health care are aware of your organ donation plans. Your spouse or some other close family member must sign a form consenting to the donation of your organs after you die. If that family member is unaware of your wishes or disagrees with them, the person might refuse to sign the form. Roadmap 2.2 outlines the basic steps in preparing a health care directive.

Durable Power of Attorney. It is a good idea to give someone a durable power of attorney in addition to giving someone the power to make health and medical care decisions on your behalf. This person would help manage your financial and business affairs if you are unable to do that because you are too ill or too injured. The person to whom you give the power of attorney for your health care does not need to be the same person as the one to whom you gave a durable power of attorney because each job requires different skills.

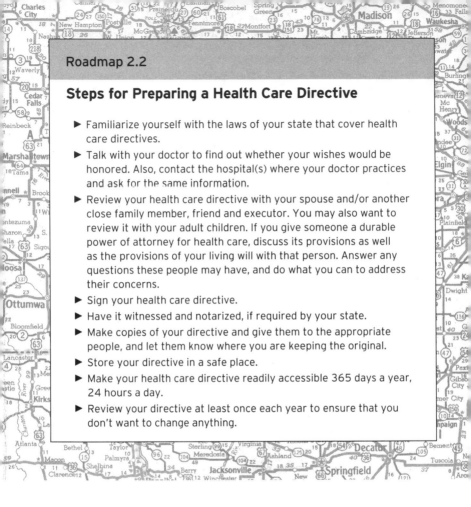

Roadmap 2.2

Steps for Preparing a Health Care Directive

► Familiarize yourself with the laws of your state that cover health care directives.

► Talk with your doctor to find out whether your wishes would be honored. Also, contact the hospital(s) where your doctor practices and ask for the same information.

► Review your health care directive with your spouse and/or another close family member, friend and executor. You may also want to review it with your adult children. If you give someone a durable power of attorney for health care, discuss its provisions as well as the provisions of your living will with that person. Answer any questions these people may have, and do what you can to address their concerns.

► Sign your health care directive.

► Have it witnessed and notarized, if required by your state.

► Make copies of your directive and give them to the appropriate people, and let them know where you are keeping the original.

► Store your directive in a safe place.

► Make your health care directive readily accessible 365 days a year, 24 hours a day.

► Review your directive at least once each year to ensure that you don't want to change anything.

You can give someone a durable power of attorney that applies to either your general person or your business affairs. It can also be set up to apply to a specific transaction. Regardless of what kind of power of attorney you give someone, you must do it while you are mentally competent and understand your actions.

If your estate is modest and you want to make sure that your personal or business affairs will be well managed if you become incapacitated, a durable power of attorney can be an inexpensive alternative to establishing a trust and naming a trustee to manage your affairs. In fact, a durable power of attorney is sometimes called a poor man's trust.

If you don't give someone a durable power of attorney and you become unable to manage your own affairs, your family can ask the court to appoint a guardian for you. However, like the appointment process for a conservator, the court process can be expensive and emotionally difficult for your family. It can also take time, leaving your affairs in limbo until a guardian is appointed. Also, the person the court appoints as your guardian may not be someone you would want making decisions for you if you could speak on your own behalf.

▶ Choosing Travel Companions: Naming Your Beneficiaries

Your beneficiaries are the individuals, organizations, and others to whom you leave your property. They can include your spouse and children, other family members, your unmarried partner, your close friends, your alma mater, a favorite charity, a cherished pet, and so on. Your beneficiaries may or may not be your legal heirs—the relatives who the laws of your state say are entitled to inherit from you if you do not write a will.

Deciding what you want to leave to each of your beneficiaries may seem like a simple task that you can accomplish quickly. Even so, you should not rush through those decisions if you want to be sure that you leave your assets to those who you most want to receive them and those who will benefit from and/or appreciate them the most. Therefore, spend some time thinking about what you own and what you want to accomplish through your will. You should also consider whether any of your decisions may cause problems or conflicts for your beneficiaries and how to deal with them. In addition, you may want to consider the possible consequences of giving a certain asset to a particular person, charity, and so on. To help you think about these issues, ask yourself:

1. Who do I want as my beneficiaries?
2. Do any of them have special needs?
3. Do I want to treat all of my children the same, or do I have good reasons to treat them differently?
4. Do I want to leave everything to my spouse? Will I create tax problems for my spouse if I do that? What can I do now to avoid or minimize those problems?

5. Do I want my beneficiaries to have full control of the assets I leave them when I die or as soon as they turn age 18 or 21?
6. How can I ensure that the children from another marriage will receive some of my property when I die?
7. Is my spouse a responsible money manager or will all my money be frittered away and would my assets end up in a financial mess?
8. Are any of the gifts I want to leave to a particular beneficiary likely to spark controversy and discord among my heirs, maybe even a contest to my will? What can I do to avoid these problems?
9. Can I make someone's life happier and/or more secure with a special gift?

Your answers to these and any other questions you think of may suggest that you should use other estate planning tools besides a will. For example, if you do not want your daughter to gain full control over the assets you are leaving her once she becomes a legal adult, you may want to place those assets in a trust for her and use the trust document to spell out exactly when your daughter should have control of the assets you place in the trust (see Chapter 5).

Whenever you designate a beneficiary for a specific asset, you should name an alternate beneficiary too. That way, if your primary beneficiary dies, your alternate will get it instead.

Rather than naming a specific beneficiary for each asset, you can leave certain types of assets to a particular category of beneficiary and then define exactly whom you are including within that category. This approach is especially appropriate if your children are beneficiaries of your will. For example, you could leave certain assets to "All of my children" and then name each of your children.

In addition to naming beneficiaries and alternates in your will, you should designate a residual and an alternate beneficiary. This beneficiary would receive any and all assets in your estate that you do not leave to a specific beneficiary should you overlook one or more assets when you write your will or forget to revise your will after you acquire a new asset. If you die without transferring a particular asset through your will or by using some other estate planning tool, the probate court decides which of your heirs is legally entitled to that asset.

Traveling with Your Spouse: Naming Your Spouse as a Beneficiary

If you are married and live in a community property state, you and your spouse each own an undivided one-half interest in the total value of all of your community property. Your spouse's one-half interest will be unaffected by your death and vice versa. Therefore, if you want to ensure that your spouse gets your share of the community property when you die, you must specifically name your spouse as the beneficiary of your share in your will. Otherwise, your spouse could end up sharing ownership of your community property with someone else, such as your child or perhaps another relative. Particularly if the asset is an important one, like your home or an heirloom, this kind of ownership arrangement could create problems for your spouse. For example, your spouse might want to sell the asset or borrow against it but the co-owner might disagree and prevent your spouse from doing so.

If you live in a separate property state, the law says that when you die, your surviving spouse is entitled to a fixed amount of your estate. If you don't leave your spouse at least that amount, your spouse can exercise the right to petition the court to receive the fixed amount rather than the amount in your will.

Traveling with the Kids: Naming Minor Children as Beneficiaries

All states limit the amount of property that a minor child can legally own without adult supervision. Usually, the amount is between $2,500 and $5,000. Therefore, if the value of the property you leave your young child in your will is more than your state's maximum, you must designate a property guardian for the child in your will. The property guardian will manage the property/assets on your child's behalf until the child becomes a legal adult.

Philanthropic Travel: Naming Charitable Organizations as Beneficiaries

You can use your will to give your assets to a charitable organization. You can indicate that you want the charity to use your gift for a general or a specific purpose. If the organization is an IRS-approved charity, your gift is exempt from federal gift and estate taxes and from those same taxes in most states.

If you include any charities in your will, be sure that you list each organization's complete legal name, identification number, and exact address. Otherwise, you may unintentionally benefit the wrong organization.

Traveling with Pets: Making a Furry Friend a Beneficiary

Even if you think your estate is too small to worry about any planning, have you given any thought to who will take care of your dog, cat, or other pet when you die? Do you want to make sure some of your money goes to the care of your pet?

You can remember Fido or Whiskers or some other pet in your will with restrictions. In most states, you cannot give any assets directly to a pet and you cannot set up a trust for a pet in the animal's name. However, you can leave money in your will to a family member or friend and stipulate that the funds be used to care for your pet after your death. Another more expensive way to remember your pet is to establish a trust in the name of a friend, family member, or someone else and specify in the trust document what the funds must be used for.

Travelogue: Special Messages and Explanations

You can do more with your will than designate who gets what. You can also use your will to leave behind special messages. For example, you might want to let your spouse and child know how much you love them or you might want to tell each of your family members what you most appreciate about them. If you're like most people, you may not have many valuable assets to leave to the important people in your life, so the special messages in your will can serve as your gifts—final expressions of your feelings for them. For some of the people you care about, your message may mean more than any asset you could ever leave them.

You can also make special explanations in your will. This can be a good idea if you are concerned that your will may trigger discord within your family or among your beneficiaries or maybe even generate a will contest. For example, if you do not leave each of your children the same share of your estate, or if you leave a substantial amount of money to someone who is not one of your legal heirs, you can explain why in your will. You should also provide your executor, as well as your beneficiaries and legal heirs if appropriate, with the same explanation before you die.

If the reason you are leaving someone out of your will or are giving one child much less than another involves issues that are negative or potentially embarrassing to the person being left out or receiving less than others, it is probably best not to put the explanation in your will because a will is a public document that anyone can read. Also, you risk having your estate sued for libel if you include something negative or embarrassing to someone in your will. A better approach is to provide the person involved with an explanation while you are still alive. Your executor should get the same explanation.

▶ Finding the Right Travel Agent: Choosing an Executor

An executor is the person you name in your will to act as legal representative of your estate after you die. When you appoint an executor (now often called a personal representative or administrator), it should be someone you hold in high regard and whom you select only after considering all of the responsibilities that the person will be undertaking—there is a lot an executor has to do.

What a Travel Agent Does: Duties of an Executor

An executor works with the probate court to carry out numerous tasks and is responsible for:

- ▶ Locating your will and other important papers and information. This may require a thorough search of your home, office, safety deposit boxes, and many other places to find the will and its codicils. You can make your executor's job easier if the person knows where to find this information.
- ▶ Carrying out your written instructions relating to your body, funeral, and burial arrangements.
- ▶ Arranging for the immediate needs of survivors.
- ▶ Applying to the court to probate the will or to terminate joint tenancy and for appointment as executor, usually no sooner than five days after your death. Most wills written in recent years are self-proving, meaning that you and the witnesses signed a sworn affidavit before a notary public or someone else authorized to administer oaths. If the will is not self-proving, the witnesses to your signature must be located, and they must testify to the genuineness of your handwriting.
- ▶ Posting a bond, if required.

- ▶ Applying for Letters Testamentary. These will be used to open an estate account, gather assets, distribute property, file tax returns, etc.
- ▶ Selecting an attorney to handle the estate (if necessary).
- ▶ Giving legal written notice of their appointment to heirs (no will) and devisees (by will).
- ▶ Indicating whether bond has been filed and describing to the court where papers relating to the estate are on file.
- ▶ Taking possession of estate property, as advisable.
- ▶ Notifying decedent's life insurance companies.
- ▶ Paying expenses for last illness, funeral and burial expenses, and other debts.
- ▶ Reviewing claims as they come in to determine if they are valid.
- ▶ Selling some of the estate's assets to pay off debts.
- ▶ Having real and personal property appraised.
- ▶ Preparing and filing an inventory of all your property with inheritance tax section and clerk of court, and completing the application for determination of inheritance tax (if necessary) by filing with the clerk of court.
- ▶ Publishing a notice to creditors for debts of which you may be unaware.
- ▶ Preparing and filing federal estate tax returns and state inheritance tax returns, if the estate is subject to estate and inheritance tax.
- ▶ Preparing and filing state and federal income tax returns for your last year of life and, if necessary, for the estate.
- ▶ Arranging for your heir's ongoing living expenses.
- ▶ Determining which estate assets will be needed to pay state inheritance or federal estate taxes (if due), administration expenses, and other costs of settling the estate.
- ▶ Satisfying charitable pledges in your will.
- ▶ Ascertaining the values at date of death for all of the decedent's bank accounts, and depending on circumstances, close those accounts and open an estate account.
- ▶ Depositing or investing liquid assets of the estate in federally insured, interest-bearing accounts; readily marketable securities; or other prudent investments, if funds are not needed to meet debts and expenses currently payable.
- ▶ Distributing assets as required by law of intestate succession (no will) or by your will.

These are only a few of the numerous separate and distinct duties for which an executor can be accountable. The complexity of an estate will determine other responsibilities.

Therefore, in addition to considering a person's willingness and ability to carry out a list of duties similar to these, you should also consider how that person's rational abilities might be affected by emotional factors. Many people choose their spouse as their executor; but if your spouse is in poor health or would be easily overwhelmed with the responsibilities of being an executor, then it's a good idea to choose someone else. For example, an older child, another family member, or a close friend may make a good executor.

Before you name anyone as your executor, however, make sure that your choice for the job is willing to accept it and capable of handling the responsibility, particularly if your estate is complex and quite valuable or if you are concerned that there may be problems after your death that could complicate the probate process. Don't forget to name a substitute or an alternate executor in your will. This person assumes executor duties should your first choice be unable or unwilling to act as executor after you die.

Your executor is legally entitled to be paid a fee for acting as your legal representative, which will be paid by your estate. However, you can stipulate in your will that you don't want your executor to receive a fee. Before you do, however, talk it over with the person you want as your executor. The person may not want to take on the job unless compensated for it. There is a great deal of work involved. On the other hand, if you and your executor are especially close or the person you select doesn't want or need the money, the fee may be waived.

If your state requires that your executor be bonded, you can waive that requirement in your will. If you do, there will be a little more money in your estate to go to your beneficiaries because the cost of the bond would have been deducted from it. However, some states require a cash bond if your executor lives out of state.

Professional Executors. Rather than designating a friend or relative as your executor, you may prefer to hire a professional executor for your estate. Bank trust officers and attorneys most often fill that role. However, professional executors charge a substantial amount of money for their services—money that will come out of your estate. Therefore, using a professional executor makes the most sense if your estate is large and complex; if you are concerned that your will may be contested; or if you have reason to believe that the terms of your will may trigger conflict among your family members. Choosing a professional executor is also a good idea when there is no one in your life you feel is capable of handling the job.

Co-executors. It sometimes makes sense to appoint co-executors rather than a single executor. If your estate is especially large and complex, for example, you may not want all of the responsibilities of executor to fall on the shoulders of just one person. Having a co-executor arrangement may make sense if your first choice doesn't live close nearby. If you pick a second executor who lives nearby, that person can handle the day-to-day details of administering your estate.

Hazard!

Be aware, however, that a co-executor arrangement will probably not work if the co-executors do not like one another or don't work well together. Their interpersonal problems could slow down the probate process.

Some experts suggest that if you choose a professional executor, you name a family member or close friend as co-executor. The rationale for this suggestion is that having someone work with the professional executor who is attuned to the needs and interests of your family can make the probate process easier on your loved ones.

Characteristics of a Great Agent: What to Look for in an Executor

As we've seen, your executor is responsible for carrying out many important responsibilities on behalf of your estate. Therefore, the person you choose should be conscientious, well organized, fair-minded, and not easily intimidated by family members, creditors, lawyers, legal documents, paperwork, or court bureaucracies. It is also a good idea if your executor is trusted and respected by your family and has the time to do the job. By the way, your choice for executor must be a legal adult and a U.S. citizen and cannot be a convicted felon.

There is one additional and very important quality you should look for in an executor—a willingness to do the job. An executor's responsibilities are too important to entrust to someone who does not really want to do it. Therefore, it is a good idea to review those responsibilities with your choice for executor so that you can be certain that she or he is willing and able to assume them.

After you die, the court must formally approve your executor. Although it rarely happens, the court will appoint someone to be the executor of your estate if it denies approval.

Before you write your will, consult a qualified estate planning attorney in your state to understand the specific powers your state gives to executors as well as any restrictions your state may impose on them. If you want, you may use your will to give your executor additional powers as appropriate, assuming those other powers do not violate your state's laws. Among other things, those additional powers might include the right to make real estate transactions on behalf of your estate and the right to borrow money to pay your estate's debts.

Most executors hire an estate attorney to help them through the probate process. However, the cost of this assistance can be expensive and ordinarily is paid by the estate that is being probated. Therefore, it's a good idea to talk with your executor about when legal help would be appropriate. You may also want to suggest a particular lawyer or law firm if you have a preference. However, you cannot require that your executor follow your wishes regarding legal help. In the end, it is up to your executor whether an attorney is hired and, if so, which attorney the executor finally decides to work with.

Given the important service that your executor will perform for you and your family, while you are alive you should do what you can to make your executor's future job as easy as possible. The steps you take ahead of time can also help avoid delays in the probate process and save your estate money. What to Pack: What You Can Do Now to Make Your Executor's Job Easier Later suggests some of the things you can do.

► Changing Your Itinerary: Altering or Revoking Your Will

To be truly effective, estate planning should be viewed as a dynamic activity. That is, you should review your will periodically to ensure that it continues to reflect the assets you own and your wishes for what will happen to them after you die. Also, you should be sure that it continues to reflect your current

What to Pack

What You Can Do Now to Make Your Executor's Job Easier Later

▶ Be sure your will is legally valid.

▶ Review your will with your executor. Answer your executor's questions and explain the rationale behind any unusual provisions or anything that you believe may upset your family or someone else close to you.

▶ Let your executor know where you are storing your will. If it is in a home safe or safe-deposit box, tell your executor where you keep the combination or key.

▶ Give your executor an unsigned copy of your will. If you revise your will or revoke it and write a new one, give your executor a copy of the changes or a copy of the new will.

▶ Explicitly state in your will that you expect your executor to hire professionals as needed to help him or her carry out his or her duties as executor. This statement will discourage your beneficiaries from complaining if your executor uses the services of an attorney, a CPA, an appraiser, and so on.

▶ Give your executor a copy of your estate planning worksheet. Maintain complete and well-organized records related to your personal finances, property, and investments, and let your executor know where those records are kept.

▶ Provide your executor with pertinent information regarding your personal life and family history.

▶ If you own a business or have an interest in one, make sure your executor knows the location of all pertinent records related to the business and what you want done with your business or business interest after you die.

▶ Give your executor the names, addresses, and phone numbers of your attorney, CPA, banker, financial advisors, and any other professional advisors you work with.

▶ Write out your desire for your burial or cremation as well as any specific arrangements you have made. Be as detailed as possible. Give your executor a copy. Your spouse or unmarried partner should also have a copy.

▶ If you have made arrangements to donate any of your organs after you die, put the information in writing. Include the name, address, and phone number of the organization/s you want to donate to. Give a copy of this information to your executor and to your spouse or unmarried partner.

family situation. For example, amend your will if you have a child, divorce, or sell a major asset listed in the will. Also revise your will if you acquire a major new asset like a home or move to another state. If someone you name in the will as a beneficiary, an executor, or a guardian dies, appoint another person in their place.

You can either revoke the earlier will and replace it with a new one or add a codicil, or an amendment, to the earlier will. If you issue a new will, make sure that the earlier one is destroyed. If you add a codicil, make sure that it is signed and dated so it is clear that the amendment was adopted after the will was originally drawn up. When you sign and date the will, have it witnessed by at least two, and preferably three, people with no connection to the will so you receive what is known as proof of will.

Change of Plans: Reviewing Your Will

Keep your will as up-to-date as possible, so it will reflect the changing circumstances in your life as well as the changes in the assets you own. Even if you don't think there have been any important changes in your life, review your will every one to two years. Although you may not have acquired or sold any assets, as you read your will you may realize that you have changed your mind about some of its provisions.

Rerouting Your Trip: How to Revise Your Will

You can revise your will any time you want and as many times as you want so long as you are physically and mentally competent when you make the changes. If the change you want to make is relatively minor; that is, you are not changing your entire gift-giving scheme or adding a testamentary trust to your will, for example, you can amend it by preparing a codicil. A codicil is simply a written statement of the change you are making. To be considered a legally valid part of your will, the codicil must be dated, witnessed, and notarized according to the laws of your state and it must be kept with your will.

You can write an unlimited number of codicils. However, the more codicils you write, the greater the likelihood that they will create inconsistencies, contradictions, or ambiguities in your will when they are read together. Therefore, it's best to limit the number of codicils to just two per will. If you want to write more than two codicils, revoke your current will and write a new one.

Re-ticketing: Revoking Your Will

If you prepare a new will, cancel your old will by declaring in the new one that you revoke all previous wills. To be safe, make this statement even if your state law says that you revoke a will simply by destroying it—by ripping it up, burning it, or defacing it, for example.

Learn the Language

Key Terms to Know When Mapping Your Trip

bond a legal document issued by a bonding or insurance company guaranteeing that if your executor, account custodian, or a trustee, fails to carry out their legal responsibilities, the company will pay a certain amount of money to whomever is harmed as a result.

codicil an amendment to your will. Generally, codicils are used to make relatively small changes to your will. A codicil is considered part of your will and to be legally valid must meet your state's legal requirements for a codicil.

community property property acquired and income earned by a couple during their marriage and owned jointly by both spouses; each spouse has a legal claim to one-half of all of the couple's property.

community property states Arizona, California, Idaho, Louisiana, Nevada, New Mexico, Texas, Washington, and Wisconsin. At the present time, the rest of the states are separate property states.

disinheritance excluding a family member from your will.

letters testamentary certificates issued by the court, after a will is admitted to probate, to the executor as evidence of executor's authority.

pour-over will a document that specifies that any or all property not specifically held in trust be transferred to the trust.

probate estate all of the assets that you own that will go through the probate process.

property guardian person you name in your will to manage the property you leave your minor child should you die before your child is a legal adult.

residuary beneficiary person named in your will who is entitled to receive any of the assets in your probate estate that are not specifically left to another beneficiary in your will after all legitimate claims against your estate have been paid.

residuary estate assets left in your estate after all the assets with specific beneficiaries have been distributed; also called the *residue of the estate.*

self-proving will a will that includes a sworn statement from witnesses that it has been notarized.

take against the will an option given to surviving spouses to inherit a state-determined amount of their deceased spouse's estate rather than whatever the deceased left them in their will.

Uniform Anatomical Gift Act promulgated in 1968 and adopted by all 50 states and the District of Columbia to standardize ethical, legal, and policy issues related to organ donation.

Negotiate Customs

How to Avoid Probate and Taxes

▶ The Road to Probate

Most people have two key estate planning goals. One goal is to ensure that as much of their estate as possible goes to their beneficiaries rather than having it depleted by probate fees, taxes, and other expenses. The other goal is to ensure that their estate transfers to their beneficiaries as quickly as possible.

Probate court will not be enjoyable for your loved ones, but it is unavoidable in some cases and in some states whether you die with or without a will. (Without a will, the process can be much more difficult and take considerably longer.) The first step in the probate process is establishing that the will, if one exists, is a valid last statement, declaring your wishes for distributing your assets and naming the guardians of your minor children, if any.

Next, the probate court appoints an executor to administer the estate. Usually, the court designates the person named in the will. If no will exists, the court assigns an administrator, often a family member. The court then oversees the executor's or administrator's work, which consists of identifying, or marshalling, all the assets; paying off all debts, taxes, and administrative costs; and, finally, disposing of the remaining assets to the beneficiaries.

A federal and state estate-tax return must be filed within nine months of death if the estate's value exceeds the lifetime estate tax exemption. If the surviving family needs money immediately to meet living expenses, the executor can distribute some income, or even principal, as needed while the probate process continues.

The executor receives a fee. The amount of the fee may be stated in the will, although the court may limit the fee to a set percentage of the estate as a commission—for example, 3 percent of your gross estate paid as a fee for administering the estate. Usually, an independent executor, such as a lawyer or bank, collects between 2 and 5 percent of the estate's value, depending on the amount of assets involved and the complexity of the case. A family member executor usually charges far less than an independent one or may refuse to accept a fee out of love for the family. However, dealing with the conflicting demands of family members can be a thankless job and one well worth the remuneration.

All fees—which can amount to thousands of dollars—are paid by the estate. If the will is clear, with no one contesting it, the executor can distribute the assets. Usually, executors like to pass on actual physical assets to beneficiaries, whether the assets are tangible or intangible. However, this is not always possible. For example, an executor might have to sell some assets to raise cash to pay creditors or for estate taxes. Once all assets are distributed and all taxes are paid, the executor closes the estate. This may require filing a form with the court, which must approve everything the executor did. If the court and beneficiaries receive no challenges to the disposition of the estate, the matter is closed.

The probate process lasts from several months to several years. One disadvantage of probate, in addition to its slowness, is that all proceedings are public. The court may even require that certain notices be placed in newspapers to ensure that potential beneficiaries or creditors know that the will is being probated. Because your will becomes a matter of public record, certain personal and financial details about you or your family might be revealed that you would rather be kept private.

Bumps in the Road: Potential Drawbacks of Probate

When people hear the word probate, a lot of negatives come to mind. Most people think of the probate process as expensive—the national average cost of probate is 6 to 10 percent of the value of the estate, excessively time-consuming for an executor, and needlessly slow in transferring property to the beneficiaries of a will. With the right planning, however, you can eliminate most of the negatives or at least minimize their impact. For example, although the duration of the probate process tends to vary from six months to one year, the duration can be longer or shorter depending on such factors as these:

▶ The number, value, and complexity of the assets in your probate estate
▶ The number of beneficiaries in your will
▶ Whether anyone contests the validity of your will or challenges one of its provisions
▶ The number of creditor claims against your estate
▶ The probate laws of your state
▶ The efficiency of the court that oversees your estate's probate process
▶ Whether your estate must file an estate tax return (if it does, it could take as long as two to three years before everything is settled with the IRS)
▶ Whether your will can be located immediately after your death
▶ If the witnesses to the signing of your will can't be found or, if they are not alive at the time of your death, whether there is a self-proving affidavit
▶ How long it takes to locate, value, and liquidate, if appropriate, the assets in your estate

Open Road: Potential Benefits of Probate

For all the negatives associated with the probate process, there are also benefits. First, the process helps ensure that only those individuals or organizations with true claims to your estate will get your property after you die. Second, it protects your estate by limiting the amount of time that creditors with claims against it can try to get paid by your estate. The period of time is usually somewhere between four and six months. Creditors that don't present their claims before the end of this period cannot take collection action against your estate.

How Much Does this Trip Cost?

The expenses probate entails may include among other things court costs, appraisal costs, fees paid to your executor, and attorney fees—but there are ways to minimize your estate's probate costs. For example, by carefully planning your estate and by writing a legally valid and clearly worded will, you decrease the potential that problems will crop up during the probate process that will cost your estate money to resolve.

Another way to keep your probate costs down is to select a competent executor who can do some of the work that an attorney would otherwise do. In fact, if your estate is relatively small and simple and if the probate process goes off without a hitch, your executor may not need an attorney's help at all because the executor's job will be mainly pulling together information and filling out forms. Nonetheless, nearly every executor uses an attorney for at least some aspect of the probate process. In fact, not using one can be penny-wise and pound-foolish because an attorney may be able to save an executor time and money.

Another strategy for reducing the costs of probate is to pass as much of it as possible over or outside your will rather than under it. This strategy can be especially cost-effective if your state uses the value of an estate to determine the estate's probate fees.

Court Costs. In most states, the probate related court costs that an estate must pay are relatively insignificant, maybe just a few hundred dollars at the most. Those costs may include filing fees, registration fees, publication fees, and fees based on the value of your probate estate.

Appraisal Costs. Appraisal costs during probate pay for the process of valuing the property in your probate estate. Usually, an appraiser is used to place a value on assets other than cash, publicly traded securities, and similar assets—real estate, closely held businesses, fine antiques, expensive jewelry, or rare stamps, for example. If your estate is modest, appraisal costs may range from a few hundred dollars to a few thousand, depending on the amount and types of assets. However, those costs can be a lot more if there are many assets to appraise or if some of your assets are unusual and must be appraised by a specialist.

Fiduciary Fees. Fiduciary fees are the fees to which your executor is entitled; court-appointed administrators are also entitled to those fees. States limit how much an executor can receive in fees, and the fees must be approved by the probate court before they can be paid. As mentioned, family members and close friends who serve as executors often waive the right to receive any fees for their services to your estate.

Fiduciary fees are either calculated as a percentage of the net value of your estate or are determined on the basis of "reasonableness," as defined by your state. If they are based on an estate's net value, that value is the total appraised value of all the property in your estate less the total amount of debt that is secured by that property.

Attorney Fees. Attorneys typically charge for their services on an hourly basis, and there is a wide range in their hourly rates—anywhere from about $180 an hour to more than $400 an hour. In part, an attorney's rate depends on whether your estate is being probated in an urban or rural area and on the East or West Coast or anything in between. The rate is also determined by the attorney's level of experience. Seasoned attorneys tend to charge more per hour than relative newcomers to the legal profession.

Stops along the Way: How Probate Works

When people are faced with the probate process, they tend to have one of three goals:

▶ to avoid the delay and cost of probate entirely;
▶ to minimize the number of assets in their estate that must go through probate; or
▶ try to qualify for the more informal probate process if it is available to them.

Even though the formal probate process varies from state to state, the following overview is typical of the process.

Stop 1. After you die, the person you name in your will as your executor files paperwork with the probate court in your area.

Stop 2. Usually, the court formally appoints that person as executor. The court also makes sure that your will is legally valid. If you did not write a will, it appoints an administrator to do what an executor would do on behalf of your estate.

Stop 3. Your executor presents the court with a list of your assets and debts.

Stop 4. Your executor formally notifies your legal heirs as well as your creditors of your death. Your heirs and creditors will have a set amount of time—usually several months—to file claims against your estate. It is during this period that a disgruntled heir might contest the validity of your will. If no claims are filed against your estate and no one contests the validity of your will, the court will formally approve your will and admit it to probate.

Stop 5. Your executor prepares and files a final list of the assets in your probate estate, files tax returns if necessary, and gets ready to transfer those assets to your beneficiaries according to the instructions in your will.

Stop 6. Your estate pays all legitimate creditor claims, including the claims of taxing authorities that filed their claims within the allotted period of time. If your executor contests the validity or amount of a claim, this step may take considerable time to complete. None of your beneficiaries will receive the assets you have left them until this process is finished.

Stop 7. Your executor completes all final paperwork, prepares a final report for the court, and petitions the court to close your estate. This won't happen until all required fees and expenses have been paid and all issues related to your estate have been resolved. Your legal heirs can contest the executor's final accounting; if they do, the court holds a hearing.

Stop 8. The probate judge formally closes your estate and releases your executor from any further duties.

The Family Allowance. Most states allow a surviving spouse and any dependent children you had together to receive a family allowance while your estate is being probated. The allowance, which is paid by the executor out of the estate's assets, helps ensure that your family does not suffer financially during the process.

The amount of a family allowance varies from state to state. Some states pay a set amount regardless of family size or other factors. Others consider a number of factors when deciding on the amount of a family allowance. Typically, those factors include the overall financial status of the surviving spouse and the number of dependent children. Some states also protect a surviving spouse and minor children from losing their homestead to creditors. These states also prohibit the heirs or beneficiaries of the deceased spouse from forcing the surviving spouse to move out of the homestead, even if it has been left to the deceased's heirs or beneficiaries in full or in part.

In some states, the probate process has been streamlined and simplified. If you own less than $50,000 in assets, your estate may qualify for expedited treatment, which will save legal and executor fees.

Remember, only those assets in your estate that pass under your will go through probate. These assets include:

► All assets you own in your own name
► Your share of any assets you own as a tenant in common

► One-half of your community property, if you own property in a community property state
► Life insurance death benefits when your estate is the beneficiary
► Property placed in a testamentary trust

Therefore, one strategy for reducing the time and expense of probate is to maximize the assets you own that don't have to be probated. Assets that do not go through probate include:

► Jointly owned property—property that you own as a joint tenant with right of survivorship or as a tenant by the entirety
► Inter vivos gifts
► Assets placed in trust accounts
► Death benefits from IRAs, life insurance policies, and employee benefits plans as long as your estate is not the beneficiary
► Property placed in a living trust
► Some business property controlled by contracts
► Depending on your state, community property that goes to a spouse

It is important that you discuss your estate vis-à-vis the probate process with your attorney.

Shortcuts: Alternatives to Formal Probate

People are attracted by any alternative that is faster, cheaper, and more private than probate court. Avoiding probate may be desirable, but it takes a great deal of planning and thorough understanding of estate-planning rules.

If probate is a concern to you, your planning should focus on reducing the assets in your estate that will go through probate. If estate taxes are an issue for you, your planning should involve minimizing the size of your taxable estate. If your estate is small enough, your planning should ensure that the estate qualifies for the quicker and cheaper alternative to the traditional probate process that may be available in your state.

In most states, eligible estates can use an alternative to the formal probate process. Eligible estates have the following characteristics:

► They are worth a relatively small amount of money.
► They do not include any complex assets.
► There are few beneficiaries in the will.
► They have few creditors.

▶ They are not liable for estate or inheritance taxes.

Because the court's involvement is minimal in the alternative probate process, the process is faster and less expensive than the formal probate process. Although their specifics vary from state to state, the alternatives to that process tend to be one of two types: summary administration or collection by affidavit. The highlights of each process are described below.

Summary Administration. Any estate that has an executor, is valued at less than a state-set maximum—usually no more than $50,000—and that meets other state criteria is eligible.

How it works. The executor immediately transfers assets in the will to the appropriate beneficiaries and files a formal accounting with the court. Intermediate steps, such as the notification of creditors, the creditor waiting period, and the formal inventory and appraisal of probate assets, are eliminated.

Restrictions. The consent of all beneficiaries to a will may have to be obtained for summary administration to be used.

Collection by Affidavit. Any estate whose net value is less than an amount set by the state is eligible.

How it works. Whoever thinks that they are entitled to certain personal property of the deceased completes an affidavit stating so, and the holder of the property transfers it to the person who completed the affidavit.

Restrictions. Some states allow only spouses and children to collect by affidavit; others permit only certain types of property to be collected by affidavit; and still other states mandate a minimal amount of court involvement.

▶ Minimizing Tolls: Strategies to Reduce Your Estate Taxes

When you die, your estate may have to pay taxes. The more taxes it must pay, the less will be left to be distributed to your beneficiaries. Therefore, for those with substantial estates, tax minimization is an important part of estate planning. Depending on your state, taxes may be an issue even if your estate is not worth a lot.

Following are some of the taxes your estate may have to pay.

1. *Estate income tax.* Your estate must pay this tax if the income it earns in any tax year exceeds the standard exemptions an estate receives.
2. *Personal income tax.* This is the tax due on your income in the year of your death.
3. *Federal estate tax.* Your estate must pay this tax only if its value exceeds a certain dollar amount. The amount is based on the current market value of all the assets in your estate, not just those that go through probate. The amount is known as the unified tax credit.
4. *State estate tax.* A few states have their own estate taxes, although those states are growing fewer and fewer in number. Although these states may impose their tax on estates valued at less than the federal estate tax threshold, potentially affecting more modest estates, the good news is that their tax rates are considerably lower than the federal government's.
5. *The inheritance tax.* Some states tax the inheritance a beneficiary may receive. The tax is levied against the value of the inheritance, but a trend is growing among the states to eliminate this tax.

If it appears that your estate will owe taxes, there are ways to reduce that liability or even wipe it out. If your residuary estate does not have enough money to pay all of the taxes your estate owes, payment of those taxes will be apportioned among all of the assets in your estate, starting with general bequests and then moving to specific bequests. Cash, investment assets, and personal property will be tapped before real property. As a result, your beneficiaries may end up with less than what you had intended them to receive.

Unless all estate-related taxes are paid to the IRS, the agency will use any of the tools available to it to collect its money, including seizing assets and levying bank accounts. Determine your best strategy in consultation with your attorney.

If you are married, there is another way to save on taxes.

Drive Now, Pay Later: Unlimited Marital Tax Deduction

The unlimited marital tax deduction gives married people a break on their federal estate taxes. It allows you to leave all of your estate to your spouse, without incurring any estate tax liability regardless of your estate's value. Note: You must be legally married and your spouse must be a U.S. citizen to qualify.

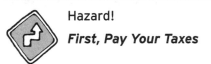

Hazard!

First, Pay Your Taxes

The taxes your estate may owe must be paid before your beneficiaries can receive what you have left them. If you made special provisions in your will for paying your taxes, your executor will follow them. Otherwise, your executor will use the money in your residuary estate to pay your taxes.

Although this deduction provides an undeniable immediate benefit to your surviving spouse, without the right estate planning it can create future tax problems for your spouse's estate because your unified estate tax credit was never used. The unified tax credit is a credit that each citizen may apply against a certain amount of assets when they die. In 2006 that limit is $2 million. If your surviving spouse owns assets in their own name, and if the assets you leave your spouse appreciate after your death, your spouse's estate could face a substantial tax liability.

If you feel that using the unlimited marital deduction may create future tax problems for your spouse, talk with an estate planning attorney. The attorney may recommend that you set up a trust to get around the problem.

So why use a marital trust?

1. It provides income to the surviving spouse for life.
2. It gives the spouse discretion to access trust principal.
3. It allows the spouse the discretion to direct assets to anyone they choose (a general power of appointment).
4. It avoids probate costs and lengthy delays.
5. It provides for a successor trustee if the spouse no longer can handle financial affairs.

▶ Side Trips: Strategies for Avoiding Probate and Taxes

Depending on the value of your estate and on your estate planning goals, you may want to do more than write a will. Therefore, understanding the range of tools available will help you make informed decisions.

Roadmap 3.1 summarizes the key advantages and disadvantages of each estate planning tool compared with a will.

The Gift of Travel: Living (Inter Vivos) Gifts

Though giving away your assets to avoid probate may sound simple enough, it isn't. Years ago, people signed over their assets to their children on their deathbed to avoid estate taxes. Since then, government rules have tightened considerably. Today, many people give away some of their assets while they are still alive. Such gifts to beneficiaries are called inter vivos gifts. If appropriate to your situation, you can also make a trust the recipient of an inter vivos gift.

Currently, federal law allows you to give up to $11,000 in money or other assets each year to as many individuals or charities as you want without triggering a gift tax, assuming your inter vivos gifts meet certain criteria. If you and your spouse make the inter vivos gifts together, you can give a total of $22,000 to each beneficiary each year without concern about the tax implications of your gifts. The amount is indexed for inflation, so check with the IRS or your accountant or tax attorney. These annual exclusion amounts must be used each year, or they are lost.

While this rather low limit on annual gifts might make it difficult to dispense your assets, giving away assets might also be troublesome if you need to live on them. Because you don't know how long you will live, you don't want to impoverish yourself by jettisoning your assets too soon. If you give gifts to relatives who are named in your will, add a provision that these gifts should not be considered advances on their inheritance. Otherwise, your gifts could be deducted from their share of your assets upon your death. If you give $100,000 to a sister who needs money for a down payment on a house, for instance, she might receive $100,000 less than you wanted her to have when you die unless that provision instructs your executor not to subtract the $100,000.

Most large gifts must be transferred to recipients at least three years before your death. If you die before the three years have lapsed, the gifts will probably be added to your estate, which might trigger the estate taxes you wanted to avoid. As we've already discussed, estate tax law has allowed husbands and wives to make unlimited gifts of property to each other under the gift tax marital deduction, which allows you and your spouse to balance

Roadmap 3.1

Key Estate Planning Tools: Advantages and Disadvantages

Will

Advantages

- ▶ Easy and relatively inexpensive to prepare
- ▶ Allows you to name a personal and a property guardian for a minor child
- ▶ Can be modified at any time up to your death

Disadvantages

- ▶ Property in a will is subject to probate
- ▶ A minor automatically receives the asset(s) at 18 or 21, depending on your state.

  You can get around this drawback, however, by using your will to set up a testamentary trust for the minor and specifying at what age you want the minor to receive that property.

- ▶ Probate often time-consuming and expensive

Joint Tenancy

Advantages

- ▶ Inexpensive and simple to use
- ▶ Avoids probate

Disadvantages

- ▶ Assets are subject to creditors of the joint tenant
- ▶ Lack of full control over an asset you own as a joint tenant
- ▶ Gift taxes may be involved in making a solely owned asset a joint asset

Living (Inter Vivos) Gift

Advantages

- ▶ Helps reduce the size of an estate for probate and tax purposes
- ▶ Provides an opportunity to see your gift used and appreciated

Disadvantages

- ▶ Lose use of the property you give away

Life Insurance

Advantages

- ► Safe, secure way to build an estate
- ► Avoids probate
- ► No income tax liability associated with benefits
- ► Good way to provide liquidity for estate

Disadvantages

- ► No flexibility governing when and how death benefits are paid to the beneficiary(s) of your policy (You can deal with this disadvantage by making a trust the beneficiary of those proceeds. In the trust document you can spell out when and under what conditions the trust's beneficiary can receive the money.)

Employee Benefits

Advantages

- ► Death benefits avoid probate

Disadvantages

- ► No flexibility in how probate benefits are paid to the beneficiary(s) of your benefits
- ► Have tax consequences

Informal Bank Trust (POD and TOD) Accounts

Advantages

- ► Usually are revocable
- ► Inexpensive and easy to set up
- ► Account funds avoid probate

Disadvantages

- ► No flexibility in how or when account funds are paid to beneficiary

Testamentary Trust

Advantages

- ► May provide tax advantages
- ► You can control when trust beneficiary receives trust assets
- ► Not established until you die

Disadvantages

- ► Trust assets go through probate before reaching trust

Revocable Living Trust

Advantages

- ► Avoids probate
- ► You have control of trust assets while you are alive
- ► You can be both trustee and beneficiary of the trust
- ► You can control when a trust beneficiary receives trust assets and income

Disadvantages

- ► Relatively expensive to set up
- ► No tax advantages unless you go to the extra expense of combining a revocable living trust with a second trust that is designed to save on estate taxes

Irrevocable Living Trust

Advantages

- ► Avoids probate
- ► May provide tax advantages (generally set up for this purpose alone)
- ► You can control when a trust beneficiary receives trust assets and income

Disadvantages

- ► Relatively expensive to set up
- ► Once an asset is placed in an irrevocable trust, it can't be removed or changed in any other way

your assets among both of your estates to take maximum advantage of the unified tax credit you each can pass on to heirs estate-tax-free.

Another way to use gifts is to dispense assets that you believe will appreciate sharply in value. For example, say you give your child 100 shares of a growth stock, which your child receives with your tax cost. Any future appreciation would be taxed only when your child sells the stock. You also may give assets that have appreciated sharply to a charity. The charity can sell the asset without paying capital gains tax, and you may take a charitable deduction. The gift proceeds may be used to purchase insurance, establish a wealth replacement trust, or provide you with lifetime income (see Chapter 4 for more information about insurance trusts).

Once your gifts exceed the excluded amounts, you will incur gift taxes, which may be eliminated or reduced by your estate tax exemption. You must use your estate tax exemption if any portion of it remains.

To be considered an inter vivos gift, an asset must be

- ▶ *A present interest in something.* Giving someone a future interest in an asset you own is not an inter vivos gift.
- ▶ *Irrevocable.* In other words, you cannot take the gift back.
- ▶ *A completed gift.* You must give up all ownership rights to the asset and cannot control it in any way.

To make sure that an inter vivos gift provides you with the estate tax reduction benefits you anticipate, you must be sure to take care of all the necessary legal paperwork. For example, if you give away real property or a car, you must change the name of the owner on all the ownership documents, give them to the new owner, and file the required paperwork with the registrar of deed or court in the new owner's name. If the gift is intangible, such as stocks, bonds, or bank accounts, you must provide the new owner with the investment certificates or passbooks for the accounts, if applicable, and make sure that the new owner's name appears on the account statements as owner going forward.

When you write your will, you may want to specify that the value of any inter vivos gifts you have already given to any of your beneficiaries should not be treated as an advance on what you've left them in your will. If you don't stipulate this, it is possible that your beneficiaries will not receive all that you intend for them to have through your will. This same advice also applies to trusts.

Advantages of Gifting. By properly gifting assets while you are alive, you can

- ▶ Experience the pleasure of giving while you are alive and of knowing how much the recipients of your gifts benefit from and appreciate them.
- ▶ Minimize the value of the assets in your estate that will go through probate so that the probate process can be completed more quickly or so that your estate can qualify for an alternative probate process (if available in your state).
- ▶ Minimize the size of your taxable estate because the asset you give away as an inter vivos gift is no longer part of your estate and therefore not

liable for estate taxes, thus potentially saving your heirs thousands of dollars in estate taxes that would be due on your death.

Tax Consequences of Gifted Property. When determining the value of a gift for tax purposes, use its value at the time it's given—not what you paid for it. Let's say that in 2001, you purchased 100 shares of stock for $10. You wish to gift all 100 shares (now worth $45/share) to your grandchild. The gift will be valued at $4,500 for gift tax purposes. Remember that you also are passing an income tax burden to the recipient of the stock. Therefore, if you gave the stock to your grandchild who sold it, the long-term capital gain would be $3,500. Making this gift may save taxes if your grandchild is in a lower tax bracket and can take advantage of the lower capital gains rates upon its sale or lower income tax rates on future dividends.

Gifts to Minors. The rules for gifting to a minor are similar; however, because minors are not of legal age, they cannot deal with their own property. Instead, an adult as custodian or trustee for the minor's benefit must own the property. Here are a few ways to gift to minors.

Gifts to Trusts. A trust is a contract through which a person deposits and holds money, securities, or other assets for the ultimate benefit of another person. When transferring property to a trust, it is usually important for the gift to qualify for the annual gift tax exclusion ($11,000 in 2005).

Transfers to a custodian under the Uniform Transfers to Minors Act (UTMA) or the Uniform Gift to Minors Act (UGMA). Establishing either account or transfer is simple. As a donor, you may transfer money, securities, and insurance contracts under the UGMA. Under the UTMA, which has been adopted in many states, you also may transfer real and personal property, partnership interests, and other property interests.

For gifts of cash or securities, banks and brokerage firms have the documents available. You will need to choose a custodian, other than yourself, to manage the property until the minor dies or reaches the age of majority (18 or 21, depending on your state). At that time, the property must be turned over to the minor or the minor's estate. The assets placed in the account qualify for the annual gift tax exclusion, and the gift is irrevocable at the time of the transfer.

The main advantages to an UGMA account are its simplicity, low cost, and ease of administration. Potential disadvantages include its inflexible distribution requirement at the age of majority, inability to transfer certain assets to such accounts, tax consequences for the child, and your irrevocable loss of control over the assets.

Types of Gifts

Cash. It must be deposited in the recipient's bank by December 31 to be counted as a current-year gift.

Joint tenancy. Generally, when you transfer property ownership from yourself alone to you and one or more other people as joint tenants, it's considered a gift. One exception: It's not deemed a gift when a joint bank account is established. A gift, however, can be made indirectly through a joint bank account when a noncontributing joint tenant makes a withdrawal. For example: Mom adds daughter's name to her checking account. Daughter withdraws $5,000 to purchase a car for herself. Mom has just given daughter a $5,000 gift (indirectly). Special note of caution: Care should be taken when transferring property into joint tenancy with someone who is not your spouse. Check with an attorney or CPA to determine the gift tax issues related to the specific property you want to transfer. (Joint tenancy is discussed in greater detail later in this chapter.)

Securities—stocks, bonds, mutual funds. This entails more paperwork. Your broker or mutual fund company will want your signature on paperwork to initiate the transfer, and the recipient will need to have a brokerage account established to take receipt of the stock.

Real estate. How you transfer real estate depends on a state's laws. Check with an attorney to make sure the deed is correctly done, particularly if you are giving a partial interest in real estate.

Insurance policy. You can transfer ownership of an insurance policy.

Crummey Trust. You can transfer any type of property into a Crummey Trust. When it's transferred, the trust beneficiary is notified of the gift and has a short period of time to request that the property be given to the beneficiary directly. This gives the beneficiary a present interest in the property and permits the gift to qualify for the $11,000 annual exclusion. If the property is not withdrawn, the property stays in the trust, and the beneficiary will have a continuing interest in the trust. Crummey Trusts frequently hold life insurance policies.

Family business. If you have a family business and would like your children to have some ownership, you can gift to them an interest in the entity. If you are a sole proprietor, you will need to establish an entity (such as a corporation) before you can make gifts. You also will need to have the entity valued by an appraiser before you make the gift.

The Family Limited Partnership (FLP) is an excellent estate planning and income tax reduction tool, if used properly. Many estate planning professionals suggest that you gift small limited partnership shares ($11,000 worth per year or less, so that no gift tax is due) to your children every year, so that the size of your taxable estate is reduced on your death. Control of the assets during your life is still retained by virtue of your spouse's general partnership interest. The value of your remaining interest is further reduced for estate tax purposes, because it is not a controlling interest. (After all, who would buy the share for full value on the open market?)

It is best to work with your attorney or CPA on this type of gift, as several issues need to be addressed when transferring ownership of a family business. (Estate planning and your business are reviewed in depth in Chapter 6.)

Additional Gift Exclusions. The tax code allows two additional gift exclusions.

Tuition payments. You may pay tuition expenses directly to a qualifying university, college, or a technical school. The exclusion does not include other expenses such as books, supplies, dormitory, or other fees that do not constitute direct tuition costs.

Medical expenses. Also worth considering are the direct payments of medical expenses (which can be claimed for federal income tax purposes, including medical insurance).

When making these gifts, you get the added benefit of their not counting toward your annual gift amount for the year.

Charitable Gifting. There are several ways to give money to your favorite charity and at the same time benefit your estate.

The Planned Deferred Gift. In your will, living trust, IRA, life insurance contract, or any investment, name one or more of your favorite charities as beneficiary. While you're alive, you control the asset and have access to it. The plan is put in place now; the gift is deferred until after your death.

An Immediate, Outright Gift. You can make an immediate, outright gift with cash, publicly traded securities (stocks, bonds, and mutual funds), real estate, or closely held stock. The benefits to you include an immediate charitable deduction, and you bypass any capital gains tax on the appreciation of the securities, real estate, or closely held stock owned for more than one year. The charity(ies) you name would begin receiving monies immediately and in perpetuity.

A Charitable Gift of Life Insurance. If you have a good income but have not accumulated the surplus assets—above and beyond the amount you need to support yourself during retirement—but also some charitable intentions, consider purchasing a life insurance contract and naming a community trust as the owner and beneficiary of the policy. Because the charity is the owner and beneficiary, the life insurance premium is tax deductible. At your death, the full amount will be paid to your endowment fund at the community foundation. A small premium purchases a major gift or, perhaps you have an existing policy, and the current named beneficiary really could be changed to your favorite organization.

Traveling Together: Joint Ownership

Owning assets with someone else as joint tenants with right of survivorship is an inexpensive and simple estate planning tool. If you and another person own property as joint tenants, your share automatically passes to your co-owner when you die. Therefore, these assets do not need to be included in your will and do not go through probate.

Spouses frequently own such assets as a home or a bank account as joint tenants. However, you can also own property as a joint tenant with another relative, your unmarried partner, a close friend, business partner, or someone else.

Another type of joint ownership very similar to joint tenancy is tenancy by the entirety. This form of ownership, however, is only available to spouses. Real estate and bank accounts are commonly owned as tenants by the entirety.

By holding assets in joint tenancy with right of survivorship with your spouse or another when you die, this asset automatically transfers to the survivor without going through probate court. While the approach sounds simple, it has its problems, so before you rush off to make all of your assets joint assets with one of your beneficiaries as your co-owner, you should be aware of the potential drawbacks to this form of ownership:

1. You may not have full control over a joint asset. Therefore you can't sell the asset if your co-owner balks, although you or your co-owner could give away your share or even lose it all as the result of a court judgment against either party. Under such circumstances, it is possible that you

could end up losing your half of the asset as a result of a claim against your co-owner or owning a joint asset with someone you don't know should your co-owner lose his or her share in a collection action or give the share away.

2. If you no longer want to own an asset as a joint tenant, it can be extremely difficult, if not impossible, to change the nature of your ownership.

3. If you change an asset that you own by yourself into a joint asset by giving a share of the asset to someone other than your spouse, it will be viewed as an inter vivos gift. Depending on the value of the share, your estate may be subject to a federal gift tax.

4. Some states freeze the funds in a joint bank account after a joint account holder dies. To regain access to the account, the other account owner must present certain legal documents. If the other account owner is your surviving spouse and needs the funds to pay bills and/or to help pay your funeral and burial expenses, the delay created could mean a lot of hardship for your spouse.

5. Joint ownership can make it difficult for a spouse to become eligible for Medicaid. This can be a serious problem if a spouse needs long-term care and does not have private long-term care insurance. If paying for long-term care insurance may be an issue for you or your spouse in the near future, consult an attorney familiar with elder law and the rules of Medicaid before you make an asset a joint asset with your spouse or end a joint ownership arrangement. Most commonly people purchase long-term care insurance in their 50s or 60s.

6. Joint ownership can create tax problems for husbands and wives with substantial estates, particularly if both die simultaneously, in which case, your entire estate will be settled at once—and if your assets are greater than the unified tax credit, your estate will have to pay taxes. An estate planning attorney can advise you how to deal with such problems.

7. If you hold your assets in joint tenancy with a person who is not your spouse, the same estate tax consequences apply, except no marital deduction is allowed. Also, the assets will be valued in the deceased's estate for 100 percent of their value at death unless the surviving joint tenant can prove that they paid for some or all of the assets. Upon the survivor's death these same assets, if remaining, will again be subject to state taxation.

Dear Roger,

Do you remember my business partner, Rex? Well, as a result of something he's done, the government has stepped in and shut us down. Even though I didn't know what Rex was doing, I am personally responsible for paying fines and other amounts.

I wish I was telling you this because you are my brother and I need a shoulder to lean on, but you are going to be affected by this, too. Last year, we went to our lawyer and asked how you could avoid probate on your assets when you died, and she suggested putting your assets in joint tenancy—it was less expensive than a trust—with your heirs.

When you added my name to your bank accounts, we agreed that I wouldn't take any of the money out of the accounts until your death.

Who could have anticipated Rex? When the government froze all of my accounts, they froze those joint accounts, and are going to force me to use the money in those accounts to pay off the debts (I don't have enough in my own accounts). I am so sorry; I will make it up to you —even if it takes me the rest of my life.

Love,

Madelyne

Obviously, when your intended heir is in a high-risk profession, carefully consider whether you want to add their name to your accounts as a joint tenant. Madelyne was not in a high risk profession. At least, she didn't think she was, but even if the risk of losing your assets in a lawsuit is relatively low, once you add another person or more people into the mix, your risk increases exponentially.

As you can see from Roadmap 3.1, every strategy you encounter will have both pros and cons. The trick is to understand whether the pros (in

Roger's case, the cheaper cost of joint tenancy over the cost of setting up a trust) outweigh the cons (the possible loss of assets to claims of Madelyne's creditors).

Pocket Change: Life Insurance

Purchasing a life insurance policy is a very safe way to build an asset over time to provide for a beneficiary or to provide your executor with the money needed to help pay your estate's probate costs, debts, and taxes. So long as the beneficiary of your life insurance policy is not your estate, the policy proceeds will not go through probate when you die. Therefore, they will be available immediately after your death. This is one of the main advantages of insurance: It provides a source of ready cash if settling your estate drags on in probate court.

However, if your estate is the policy beneficiary, the insurance proceeds will be probated. Another potential drawback to making your estate the beneficiary of a life insurance policy is that the proceeds will be subject to the claims of any creditors you may owe money to at the time of your death. However, in most states the proceeds will be protected from those claims if you make the policy payable to your spouse, a dependent, or to a trust for the benefit of someone else, which might be best under certain circumstances.

This might be a trust you establish during your lifetime or one that springs into existence when you die. For example, if you have children younger than age 18, you might want the insurance money to go into a trust administered by a responsible trustee rather than directly to the children. Always consult a skilled insurance specialist and an estate attorney when setting up such insurance arrangements.

The main disadvantage of using an insurance policy as an estate planning tool is its lack of flexibility. For example, as the policyholder, you cannot specify when the beneficiary of your policy should receive the policy proceeds or how the proceeds will be paid—lump sum, in a series of payments, and so on. Everything is spelled out in the insurance policy.

This lack of flexibility could be a problem if the value of the policy death benefits is substantial and especially if your beneficiary is a poor money manager. The worst-case scenario is that your beneficiary may squander the policy proceeds, leaving him without enough income to live on. (See Chapter 5 for more about life insurance as part of your estate planning strategy.)

Company Travel: Employee Benefits

Employee benefits and individual retirement accounts (IRAs) are common estate planning tools. Employee benefits include pension plans, 401(k)s, annuities, profit-sharing plans, stock options, bonuses, and so on.

Typically, employee benefits plans and IRAs provide you with retirement income while you're alive and also provide benefits to your designated beneficiary after you die. To find out how and when the benefits will be paid out, read the documentation related to your employee benefits or IRA, or talk with the plan administrator.

Most retirement pension plans give your benificiary the option to start receiving benefits as soon as you die, whether or not you are retired. Because these plans take effect so quickly after you die, they avoid probate altogether. If you die once you are retired and receiving pension checks, annuity payments to your spouse, if married, and in some cases another beneficiary, if not married, can continue until their death. Check with your employee benefits department to make sure that you have chosen the options that will protect your spouse when you die.

Having the death benefits from your employee benefits plan or IRA paid to a beneficiary over time in a series of periodic payments, like an annuity, can be a good way to help that person pay the living expenses. The most common and usually the best option is for the beneficiary to roll over the assets from a qualified retirement plan or IRA directly to an "inherited IRA" account. Spouses may postpone withdrawals until the deceased would have been required to make withdrawals. All others could stretch out withdrawals over their lifetimes, thereby postponing income taxation. Generally, the death benefits do not go through probate unless you name your estate as beneficiary.

The major drawback of using an employee benefits plan or IRA as an estate planning tool is that they lack flexibility. Like a life insurance policy, you have no control over how and when your beneficiary will receive the death benefits from those assets. However, as with insurance, you can eliminate this drawback by setting up a trust to receive the benefits. We'll talk about the advantages and disadvantages of trusts in the next chapter.

Learn the Language

Key Terms to Know When Negotiating Customs

estate (death) taxes taxes your estate may have to pay after you die depending on its value.

gift tax a federal tax applied to inter vivos gifts; annual gift tax exclusion of $11,000 per recipient per year ($22,000 if you and your spouse make a gift as a couple); no limit on number of recipients in any year.

inter vivos gift a gift that you make to a beneficiary while you are alive.

irrevocable trust a trust that cannot be revoked, modified, or terminated, except as provided in the trust agreement.

joint tenancy ownership in which two or more parties hold equal and simultaneously created interests in the same property and in which title to the entire property is to remain with the survivors on the death of one of them. Married people and unmarried partners often own property this way.

marital exemption a federal tax exemption that allows one spouse to pass all of their estate to the other spouse without any estate tax implications.

revocable trust a living trust that can be modified or even canceled after it is set up.

tenancy by the entirety in some states, a form of joint ownership that is available only to spouses.

Choose Your Vehicle

Using Trusts to Achieve Your Goals

▶ Maximize Your Mileage with Trusts

A trust is a legal entity for holding assets you have earmarked for a beneficiary. Like a corporation, a trust has its own legal identity that is totally separate from yours. It has its own tax ID and pays its own taxes, just like a corporation. Except for a living, revocable trust, it is established by a legal document, called the trust agreement which defines how the trust operates, things it is and isn't allowed to do (such as distribute income to a certain person). To set up a trust you need three parties: The *grantor,* or donor, is the person whose assets are placed in trust; the beneficiary is the person or persons who receive benefits—whether income or principal—from the trust; and the *trustee* is an independent manager who administers the trust to make sure that the grantor's wishes are fulfilled. There may be one or several trustees. You may name yourself, a relative, a trusted friend or business associate, a financial professional like a lawyer or an accountant, or an institution like a bank or trust company.

A trust must be established with a formal, written, legal document. Though you may be able to write a trust with the help of do-it-yourself books or software, show the results to a qualified lawyer to make sure that you have covered all your bases legally. If you establish a more complicated trust, consult an attorney who specializes in estate planning. Though it might cost several hundred or even a thousand dollars up front, seeking this expertise could save you and your family tens to hundreds of thousands of dollars in the future.

An irrevocable trust holds assets so that, when you die, those assets will not be considered part of your estate for probate and possible estate tax purposes. A trust agreement permits you to set aside assets for the ultimate benefit of another person, called the beneficiary. In some cases, the beneficiary will receive income from the trust assets for life, while in other cases they would receive principal from the trust.

A trust is the most flexible of all estate planning tools, which is a key reason why trusts are so popular and so useful. You can set up a trust to do just about anything as long as the trust's purpose doesn't conflict with the laws of your state and doesn't promote anything that would be considered against public policy.

More than any other estate planning tool, a trust gives you control over the assets you leave to a beneficiary, even after you die. For example, you can stipulate exactly when and under what conditions the beneficiary of a trust can receive the trust assets. When you make those decisions, you take into account a beneficiary's financial needs, age, maturity, physical or mental limitations, money management abilities, and so on.

▶ Unlimited Mileage: The Flexibility of a Trust

To illustrate just how flexible a trust can be, here are some estate planning goals and an explanation of how trusts can help you accomplish each of them:

Goal: You want to provide for your child's financial needs in the event you and your spouse both die while the child is still a minor and you want to ensure that the money and other assets you leave your child will be managed to maximize their value. If you place the assets you have earmarked for your child in a trust, you can stipulate how you want the trustee to manage and use them on your child's behalf. The trustee will not necessarily be constrained by the legal restrictions and requirements that states place on property guardians.

Goal: You plan on leaving your teenage grandchildren a substantial amount of money, but you don't want them to have access to that money as soon as they become legal adults because you don't think they will be mature enough at that age to manage the money wisely. When you set up a trust for your grandchildren, you can stipulate when they will have control of the money and how much of the trust income, if any, they will receive each year up to that point.

Goal: Your child is mentally handicapped and can neither earn an income nor manage money. Therefore, you want to be sure that your child will be well cared for after you die. You can establish a trust for your child without jeopardizing any government benefits your child is already receiving or may be eligible for.

Goal: You are worried that your free-spending spouse will quickly squander everything you have bequeathed at your death. You can set up a trust that prevents your spouse from ever having unfettered access to the assets you place in the trust. Instead, the person you name as trustee will manage the assets for your surviving spouse and provide with a regular income from the trust. The trustee can also fund from the trust assets special needs and requests your spouse may have, assuming you give the trustee that power in the trust paperwork.

Goal: Your health is failing and you are concerned that in the not too distant future you may no longer be able to manage your own finances. You can set up a trust, name yourself as both trustee and beneficiary, and designate a co-trustee as well. When you are no longer able to act as trustee, your co-trustee will take over, managing the trust assets according to the instructions you have spelled out in the trust document.

Goal: You own real estate in multiple states and are worried that your executor will have to deal with the probate process in each state. You can get around this problem if you place your real estate in a trust.

Goal: You want to leave your vacation home to your three children so they can all continue to enjoy it after you die, but you are worried that there may be conflicts over its use. With a trust, you can leave the vacation home to all of your children and dictate rules for its use.

Goal: You plan on leaving all of your assets to your current spouse, but you want to be sure that a share of those assets will go to the children from your previous marriage after your spouse dies. You can address this concern with a trust.

Goal: You want to reduce your estate taxes or minimize the amount of your estate that must go through probate. Again, a trust is the answer.

Trusts can not only help you transfer assets and minimize estate taxes, they also provide far more privacy than probate court proceedings. Trust documents normally are not made public and therefore allow you to dispense assets without public disclosure.

While most of your assets can be transferred to trusts, they cannot hold everything. For example, it may be unwise to deposit the stock of a closely held corporation or stock options in a trust. Consult with a qualified estate planning attorney for guidance on closely held businesses. Nevertheless, a trust can greatly simplify the process of settling your estate.

▶ Find a Trusted Guide: The Role of the Trustee

When you set up a trust, you must designate someone to serve as its trustee. In the case of revocable living trusts, the granter generally names him- or herself and often their spouses as co-trustees first. You may choose a family member, a close friend, a lawyer, a bank trust department, or a trust company as trustee. Be sure to name an alternate or a successor trustee in case your first choice for trustee is unable to carry out the duties when the time comes.

The trustee will manage the assets you place in the trust according to the instructions you set out in the trust agreement on behalf of the trust's beneficiary. Therefore, your choice of trustee should be someone with good financial sense and sound judgment and someone you have confidence in. In some cases, such as a trust for the care of a mentally incompetent child, the trustee may have responsibility for managing the assets for many years and could therefore have a direct effect on the long-term financial well-being of your loved one.

Trustees are entitled to be compensated for their services. Usually they receive a flat fee or a fee that is a percentage of the value of the assets in the trust they are managing. The fee arrangement depends on the state where the trust is located. Although a nonprofessional trustee may waive the fee, a professional trustee will not.

▶ Fork in the Road: Types of Trusts

There are three types of trusts: informal bank trusts, testamentary trusts, and living trusts (revocable and irrevocable).

No-Frills Travel: Informal Bank Trusts

Payable-on-death (POD) accounts and Totten trusts are informal bank trusts. They are inexpensive and easy-to-establish estate planning tools. They are also practical alternatives to a formal trust for people with modest estates. The funds in these types of accounts do not go through probate.

You can establish an informal bank trust simply by opening an account in your name at a bank or at another authorized financial institution, such as a brokerage house, and designating an account beneficiary. You and your spouse or you and someone else can establish an informal trust together. While you are alive, you have use of the account funds. When you die, anything left in the account passes directly to the account beneficiary.

The primary disadvantage of an informal trust account is that you have no control over how and when the funds in the account are paid to your beneficiary. After you die, all of the account funds go straight to the account beneficiary. Therefore, you may only want to use an informal trust to transfer small amounts of funds.

Most states permit informal trusts, but some states place limits on them. You can find out how your state treats them by speaking with the appropriate person at your financial institution or with your estate planning attorney.

Economy Fare: Testamentary Trusts

A testamentary trust is relatively easy and inexpensive to set up. It is created according to the directions you lay out in your will. Prior to your death, a testamentary trust exists on paper only—in your will—and no assets are transferred into it. After you die, however, the trust comes into existence and assets you've earmarked for the trust are transferred into it to be distributed to the trust beneficiary(ies).

What to Pack: Key Details to Trust Agreement lists the key points you need to keep in mind when you are setting up a trust and signing the trust agreement.

What to Pack

Key Details of Trust Agreement

▶ Purpose of the trust

▶ Name(s) of the trust's beneficiary(ies)

▶ Name of the trustee(s)

▶ Specific powers and responsibilities you give the trustee. You can also use the trust agreement to prohibit the trustee from doing certain things.

▶ In general terms, your expectations regarding how the trustee should manage the trust's assets. For example, you can instruct the trustee to manage the assets in a manner that conserves the trust principal or to manage them to maximize the income the assets can produce.

▶ What you want done with any income the trust may generate—reinvest the income or distribute it to the trust's beneficiary(ies). You can also tie receipt of that income to stated milestones in the life of the beneficiary(ies) or state that the income can be used only for a particular purpose—to pay for a college education, for example.

▶ When you want your beneficiary(ies) to take full control of the assets in the trust, at which time the trustee's responsibilities will end.

First Class: Living (Inter Vivos) Trust

The most common technique used to avoid probate is to set up a living, or inter vivos, trust. There are two basic kinds of trusts: revocable and irrevocable. Revocable trusts can be changed or even canceled any time after they are established. For this reason, they do not remove assets from a grantor's taxable estate; the government considers those assets to be under the grantor's control. With a revocable trust, you must pay income taxes on revenue generated by the trust and possibly estate taxes on those assets remaining at your death.

Don't set up a revocable living trust until you understand its pros and cons. The advantages of a living trust are

1. It gives you maximum flexibility and control regarding when and under what conditions your beneficiary can receive the trust assets.

2. The trust provides direction if you are medically or physically unable to manage your own financial affairs while living.

3. You can be both trustee and beneficiary of a living trust, which means you can control, as well as benefit from, the trust assets.
4. You have more control over specifically how assets will transfer to heirs.
5. Estate assets are more immediately accessible to your heirs, because they are not tied up in the probate process.
6. It is harder for disgruntled heirs to challenge a living trust compared to challenging a will.
7. It maintains privacy as to the ultimate disposition of your assets.
8. Real estate titles held in another state are more easily transferred.

Its disadvantages include:

1. You still need to write a will.
2. A living trust is a relatively expensive estate planning tool compared with other tools.
3. A living trust does not protect your estate from your creditors.
4. It provides no income or estate tax advantages, although it can be combined with other kinds of trusts to save on estate taxes.

It is important to remember that a trust document is valid only when set up correctly.

Irrevocable trusts, on the other hand, cannot be altered or canceled by the grantor once they have been established. The assets placed into an irrevocable trust are permanently removed from your estate and transferred to the trust. The trust becomes a separate taxable entity that pays taxes on the income and capital gains it generates. Therefore, when you die, the appreciation of those assets is not considered part of your estate and not subject to estate taxes.

Both revocable and irrevocable trusts can help you transfer assets to beneficiaries after your death, and they can be used to hold the assets of someone who is mentally or physically incapacitated. Trusts are also useful if you want your assets held separately for young children. Upon your death, the trustee must report expenditures annually to a judge. If the trustee and the guardian of your children differ, this requirement acts as a check against the guardian's running off with your children's inheritance.

Given the time and expense involved in setting up a living trust, don't establish one until you have weighed its benefits versus its costs and then compared them to the costs and benefits of other estate planning tools avail-

Hazard!
Medicaid Benefits

Depending on your state, a living trust may damage your eligibility to receive Medicaid benefits. Medicaid is a federal-state program that provides health benefits for low-income and elderly people. Many people use Medicaid to help them pay for long-term care when they cannot continue living at home.

able to you. When you make this analysis and comparison, keep your estate planning goals in mind. You may conclude that there are easier and less expensive ways to achieve those goals.

For example, living trusts offer no tax advantages not provided by a well-written will. You have a lifetime exemption of $2 million in assets (in 2006) that you can pass on to your heirs tax free, either through a will or through a living trust. If your taxable estate is in excess of $2 million, an irrevocable trust may make sense. If one of your goals is to avoid the expense of probate, compare the cost of setting up a living trust and transferring assets into the trust with the costs your estate would incur if those assets were to go through probate. For small estates, it may not be worth it.

You can establish a living trust either by consulting self-help books or software or by hiring a qualified estate lawyer. In either case, we recommend consulting with an estate planning attorney before you set up a living trust. The attorney can help you determine whether you really need one and can also provide you with advice and information that may save you time and money if you do decide to establish a living trust. Trusts can be complicated to establish and if you don't do everything right, the trust will not help you accomplish your estate planning goals. Also, the attorney can help you coordinate the trust with the rest of your estate planning.

When you die, all the assets in the living trust automatically circumvent probate court, saving your heirs big headaches, costs, and delays. Also, if you deposit many of your assets in a living trust, you may be able to write a simpler will because you have far less to pass on through it. You should still have a pour-over will, which provides for the distribution to the trust of assets left out of the trust. Another advantage of a living trust is that it is rarely contested, in contrast to wills, which often give rise to heated debates and expensive legal wrangles.

Assets commonly placed in a living trust include wholly owned stocks, bonds, life insurance, and real estate. You cannot place a retirement account in a living trust, but you can designate a living trust as the beneficiary of that account.

Like a will, the living trust stipulates who gets what property when you die. Once you have set up a living trust, it is crucial that you transfer title of your assets to the trust. Otherwise, the trust remains an empty shell that does not serve its intended purpose. So, instead of keeping your assets in your name, you should change ownership to the "Your Name Trust." This applies to your home, your stocks, bonds, mutual funds, and bank accounts, and all your other major assets. All too often, people establish living trusts, and then fail to fund them!

When you set up a living trust, legal ownership of the assets you place in it are transferred to the trust. In other words, you no longer own them. However, in most states, you can "have your cake and eat it too" by making yourself the trustee, yourself as beneficiary of the trustee. By wearing both hats, you can maintain control of the trust assets while you are alive, use them, and also benefit from them. This option is an important advantage of a living trust.

Transferring ownership of assets to a trust can be a time-consuming process and expensive too. Among other things, the banks and title companies involved in the transfer process may want to review your trust agreement to confirm that you have given the trustee sufficient power to manage the trust assets. For this reason, many people use attorneys or financial advisors to help them with the ownership transfer process.

Support Trusts. If you have a spouse and children who depend on your income, you might want to set up a support trust. Trustees of such vehicles are instructed to provide enough money to support beneficiaries in a comfortable lifestyle. If possible, the trust should generate enough income to accomplish this goal. If the income from bond interest and stock dividends is insufficient, the trustee might spend some principal to continue to support. Usually, the trustee is reluctant to invade principal, however, because depleting it makes it more difficult to maintain a high level of income in the future.

Discretionary Trusts. A discretionary trust is similar to a support trust, except that it gives the trustee even more latitude in deciding how much income and principal must be spent to support the beneficiaries' lifestyle. The trustee must use their discretion in deciding what is fiscally prudent, even if the beneficiaries desire higher payouts.

Spendthrift trusts. If you have a child or spouse who appears to be irresponsible about money, a spendthrift trust may be right for you. In such a trust, you instruct the trustee to set strict limits on how much money can be doled out at any time and not to accede to demands for more. Such a trust may also be appropriate if the beneficiary is mentally or physically incompetent. A spendthrift trust can protect your assets against the claims of creditors if your beneficiaries get in trouble with the law or pile up debts. Typically, this trust is set up to last until the beneficiary turns 50. The thinking is that by that age, even a spendthrift will have matured!

Standby or convertible trusts. A standby trust stands ready to receive your assets at a particular time in your life. The trust remains empty until that time when it is converted into an active trust. To establish such a trust, have your lawyer draw up a durable power of attorney, which gives permission to move assets into the trust at the established time, when they will be managed for your benefit. For example, assets may be moved into the trust if you become incapacitated.

Bypass trusts (Family or Credit Shelter Trust). When a married couple's assets exceed the unified credit limit, a bypass trust may help provide for the surviving spouse and pass principal on to your children free of estate taxes. For this reason, it is one of the most important trusts in estate planning. Its purpose is to take advantage of the applicable estate tax exemption, thereby reducing the estate taxes due when you and your spouse die. Proper structuring should allow all principal to pass to your heirs without estate taxes at the death of the surviving spouse. That's because the amount transferred into the trust typically will be equal to the unified credit amount. (Because those amounts are changing, language may need to be added to a new or existing bypass trust to specify an amount, a percentage, or some other formula for determining the value of assets placed in the trust.)

To demonstrate how this works, assume that in 2006 a couple each owns $2 million in assets—$2 million in the husband's name and $2 million in the wife's name. If the husband leaves all of his assets to his wife, her estate would be hit with huge estate taxes when she dies. Instead, the husband sets up a bypass trust, which stipulates that his $2 million goes into the trust when he dies. Upon his death, his widow receives income generated by that $2 million for the rest of her life, plus the option of receiving principal if she needs it. Because she has only limited access to the capital in the bypass trust, that money is not counted as part of the marital deduction. When the wife dies, the $2 million in the bypass trust, along with her $2 million estate, pass to their heirs free of estate taxes.

Bypass trusts therefore accomplish two goals: They provide assets on which the surviving spouse can live, and they minimize estate taxes by reducing the surviving spouse's taxable estate. Bypass trusts also let you:

▶ Avoid probate costs and lengthy delays.
▶ Give your spouse discretion to access trust principal for specified needs (including health, maintenance, education, and support).
▶ Allow for a non-spousal trustee, which may protect your spouse in event of incapacity.

For these reasons, the marital trust is often used in conjunction with the bypass trust.

Q-TIP trusts. The idea behind Qualified Terminable Interest Property (Q-TIP) trusts is to make the most of your unlimited marital deduction and still control who inherits your assets after your spouse dies. While there are many uses for Q-TIP trusts, they are often used by wealthy people who have remarried and want to pass their assets on to the children of their first marriage while providing income for life to their current spouse.

When you leave assets in a Q-TIP, they are included in your estate because of the marital deduction, and your surviving spouse would be entitled to all of the trust income during their lifetime. On the death of the surviving spouse, the assets pass to the beneficiaries designated by the first spouse to die. In essence, this trust lets the decedent control the ultimate disposition of assets to beneficiaries of their choice (typically children from a previous marriage).

For example, you can set up a Q-TIP trust so that your assets will transfer into the trust when you die. (Note: Someone other than your spouse must be appointed trustee.) Upon your death, your spouse receives income generated by those assets for as long as they live, and is the only person allowed to receive income from the trust. Neither your spouse nor anyone else can give away the money. That's to prevent funds from being shifted to someone in a lower tax bracket, thereby ensuring the IRS that estate taxes will be paid on the assets in the trust when your spouse dies if the assets exceed the unified credit.

Insurance Trusts. An insurance policy on your life is not subject to income tax when you die; however, it is subject to estate tax, because the policy proceeds become part of your estate. If your beneficiary is your spouse, no taxes will be paid because of the unlimited marital deduction. Setting up an irrevocable life insurance trust can eliminate the tax burden on subsequent heirs.

Irrevocable Life Insurance Trusts (ILIT) ensure that the death benefit from your life insurance policy does not transfer into your estate, which could push the estate's value beyond the lifetime estate tax exemption threshold and trigger estate taxes. The trust receives the insurance proceeds when you die, thereby circumventing both estate taxes and probate proceedings.

You can stipulate how and when the insurance money will be dispensed to the beneficiaries. For example, you might want only the income paid to them for a few years, after which they receive the principal. Or you may want them to receive the principal immediately in a lump sum. You might also allow the trustee to use the life insurance proceeds to pay your estate taxes. This is called a wealth replacement trust.

In addition, this trust can hold many types of property and has specific provisions for holding insurance. Current insurance policies can be transferred to an ILIT. Often, however, a new policy is purchased directly by the ILIT. The reason: If you transfer an existing policy to an ILIT, you must live at least three years beyond the transfer date, or the insurance is included in your estate and taxed accordingly.

If you are considering a large insurance purchase, do not purchase the policy without first consulting an estate planning advisor. It may be best to set up an ILIT first, and then have it purchase the policy. Failure to plan properly for your insurance benefits could cost your heirs substantial amounts of money.

Charitable Trusts. To pass on assets to your favorite charitable institution, you may want to consider a Charitable Remainder Trust (CRT). You can make such an arrangement with your alma mater, a hospital, or your religious institution, or other non-profit organization recognized by the IRS.

If you deposit assets such as stocks or bonds into the trust, you receive an immediate income tax deduction for your contribution. During your lifetime, you also receive an annuity generated by the trust assets. When you die, the assets are retained by the charity. You can usually give an unlimited amount of assets to a qualified charity with no gift or estate-tax limitations. Income tax charitable deduction limitations do apply, however. It makes sense to give assets that have appreciated sharply in value so that you can benefit from a tax deduction for the fully appreciated price but do not have to pay income or estate tax on any capital gains. A charitable trust coupled with an irrevocable insurance or a wealth replacement trust can be a fantastic vehicle for saving income, gift, and estate taxes while you satisfy your charitable inclinations. Consult your tax advisor, your favorite charity, and your estate lawyer for help with these complex trusts.

Do not confuse CRTs with Charitable Lead Trusts (CLT), which provide an income stream to a designated charity first, and at the expiration of the trust, the remainder reverts to you or your heirs. CLTs usually are done in wills and revocable living trusts, so they are funded at death (they rarely are established during life).

Grantor Retained Interest Trusts. With Grantor Retained Interest Trusts (GRIT), appreciating assets may be removed from your estate, reducing the estate tax liability while allowing you to retain some benefits of ownership while you are alive. Although GRITs do not eliminate income taxes, when executed properly, they can help reduce estate tax liability.

With a GRIT, assets are transferred to a trust and heirs named to receive the assets at the end of a stated term—typically your lifetime. The transfer of the asset represents a gift valued at fair market value on the date of the transfer less your retained interest. The key to this trust is that your retained interest lowers the value of the taxable gift.

Qualified Personal Residence Trust (QPRT). This is a type of GRIT designed primarily for homes. Your residence is placed in the trust, but you continue to live there for the term of the trust. At the end of the term, the home becomes the property of your heirs. QPRTs are suitable if you own one or two appreciating homes and would like to enjoy these homes, keep them in your family, and ultimately reduce estate taxes.

The living trust names the beneficiary of the trust and appoints both you and someone else as trustee. Or, if you prefer, the document can name you as the only trustee and designate some other trustworthy person as the successor trustee to take over when you die or no longer can serve.

Learn the Language

Key Terms to Know When Choosing Your Vehicle

abusive trust a trust designated by the IRS as suspect, intending to illegally avoid income taxes.

bypass trust a type of trust used in conjunction with the unlimited marital deduction to reduce estate taxes.

inter vivos (living) trust a trust created during the life of the grantor.

land trust a revocable trust used to hold title to real estate; also known as *title-holding trust* or a *nominee trust*.

payable-on-death account (Totten trust) a trust you can use to leave funds to the account beneficiary.

settlor (donor, grantor) the formal term for someone who creates a trust.

testamentary trust a trust that is part of your will and that is not funded until your death.

testator a person who writes a will.

Travel Insurance

What You Need to Know About Life Insurance, Social Security, and Other Benefits

▶ At a Crossroad: Protecting Your Family with Life Insurance

Perhaps you know someone who missed out on going to college, who had to move out of the family home, or who had to go back to work when the children were small (or after retirement)—all because the family breadwinner died without enough life insurance. This is the first and foremost reason to buy life insurance. Insurance cannot replace you when you die—but it can replace the income you would have provided for your family. In most cases, you'll want the insurance amount to be enough to

- ▶ replace the income your family needs;
- ▶ complete your plan for funding your children's college education;

▶ pay any expenses that result from your death (typically, probate costs, medical expenses of the final illness, funeral expenses, and estate/inheritance taxes); and

▶ pay off any outstanding debts (like the mortgage or car loan).

Even if you aren't the family breadwinner, you should think about life insurance. If you are, for example, the parent who stays home to care for your children while your spouse goes to work, your death places a significant financial burden on your surviving spouse. Your spouse will have the additional expenses of child care in order to continue working—or will have to quit working to stay home with the children. In either case, life insurance could be set up to provide needed funds.

In other words, if your family or other people depend on you, you need life insurance to help them live without your support or services if you pass away. The insurance contract requires that the insurance company pay your beneficiaries a set amount, called the death benefit, if you should die for almost any reason. (For example, suicide is usually excluded for the first two years of a policy.) Your beneficiaries can receive the money in one lump sum, free of federal income taxes. The funds should be enough to replace your paycheck, cover daily living expenses, and pay your final medical bills and burial costs. In addition, the insurance proceeds should provide income for long-term needs such as retirement, estate taxes, or college costs.

Calculating the Mileage: How Much Insurance Do You Need?

The key question in buying life insurance is how much coverage your beneficiaries really need. You should determine this before you listen to insurance agents' sometimes confusing pitches or the details of different policies. Unfortunately, assessing how much is enough is not a simple process because each family is different. No general formula exists. You will require more coverage if you have several young children and a nonworking spouse, for instance, than you will if your spouse earns a good salary and you have only one child.

The first step in determining your ideal amount of insurance is to examine your current family situation and your potential family situation. The following describe a few typical family scenarios, broken down into high, medium, and low-need categories:

High Need. You will need a significant amount of insurance if you die as a:

► Working spouse married to a nonworking spouse, with children. Life insurance proceeds should pay for your family's living expenses and your children's education and should replace your income as sole wage earner.

► Working spouse married to a nonworking spouse, with no children. Your spouse should receive a death benefit that will generate enough investment income to replace your paycheck and cover their living expenses for the rest of your spouse's life, or for a specific number of years, depending on what you and your spouse want.

► Single parent. Because your children depend on you totally for both short and long-term expenses, life insurance proceeds should replace your income.

► Business owner. If you are the sole owner of a small business or are in partnership with someone else, your life insurance proceeds should replace your income for your family and enable your partner to carry on with the business. A special arrangement called a buy/sell agreement can be funded with life insurance proceeds to smooth the transition for both your family and your partner.

Medium Need. You will need some insurance if you die as a member of a:

► Dual-income household, with no children. Though your spouse may be able to survive on their own if you die, he or she may be compelled to adopt a significantly lower standard of living. The insurance benefit, if invested wisely, should permit your spouse to maintain a quality life.

► Retired couple, with self-supporting children. Assuming that you have not set aside enough money in savings and investments, life insurance proceeds should provide enough income to maintain your spouse's lifestyle.

Low Need. You will need little or no insurance if you die as a:

► Single person with no children. If no one depends on your income, you have little need for life insurance.

► Nonworking spouse, with no children, because a homemaker produces no income that needs to be replaced. However, any final expenses and the cost of replacing your domestic services may be needed. Your spouse will likely be able to maintain their standard of living if you die.

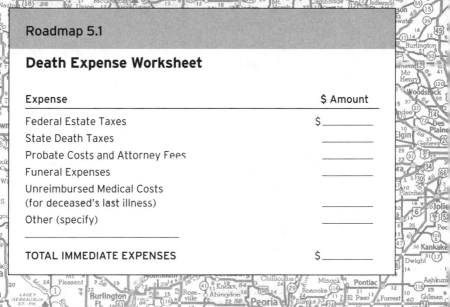

Roadmap 5.1

Death Expense Worksheet

Expense	$ Amount
Federal Estate Taxes	$ _____
State Death Taxes	_____
Probate Costs and Attorney Fees	_____
Funeral Expenses	_____
Unreimbursed Medical Costs (for deceased's last illness)	_____
Other (specify)	_____
_____	
TOTAL IMMEDIATE EXPENSES	$ _____

▶ Young child. While the insurance on children is inexpensive, it is usually unnecessary because they do not support anyone—unless they happen to be supermodels or famous child actors.

As you can see, the common thread in determining need in all of these situations is whether survivors will have enough money to maintain their quality of life if the insured dies. Calculating how much insurance you need is where this whole process can get very complicated. For an exhaustive analysis, consult your financial advisor, or a good insurance agent, or run through some of the exercises available on software like Microsoft Money or Quicken.

No matter what route you take, you will start by using Roadmap 5.1. Total the immediate expenses your family would incur if you were to die today.

Next, determine your family's ongoing future income and expenses if you were to die. The worksheet in Roadmap 5.2 provides you with space to record one year's net cash flow, but you must project this amount many years into the future if your family is young. When calculating income, include any benefits your family might be entitled to, due to your death, from government

Roadmap 5.2

Survivor's Worksheet

Income	Annual $ Amount
Benefits Income	
Life Insurance	$_____
Pensions	_____
Social Security	_____
Trusts	_____
Veterans	_____
Other	_____
Investment Income	
Annuities	_____
Dividends (from stocks, mutual funds)	_____
Interest (from bank accounts, bonds, mutual funds)	_____
Rent (from owned real estate)	_____
Other	_____
Survivor's Salary	_____
Other Income	_____
TOTAL ANNUAL INCOME	$_____

Expenses	
Child Care	$_____
Children's Education	_____
Clothing	_____
Entertainment and Recreation	_____
Food	
At Home	_____
Outside the Home	_____

Housing
  Mortgage   _____
  Rent   _____
  Utilities   _____
  Other   _____

Insurance Premiums
  Auto   _____
  Disability   _____
  Health   _____
  Life   _____
  Other   _____

Loan Repayments   _____

Medical and Dental _____

Taxes
  Federal Income _____
  State Income   _____
  Local Income   _____
  Property   _____
  Other   _____

Transportation   _____

Other Expenses   _____

TOTAL ANNUAL EXPENSES $_____

Total Annual Income $_____

Minus Total Annual Expenses $(_____)

Equals

TOTAL NET CASH FLOW $_____

programs, such as Social Security and veteran's survivor's programs, as well as from life insurance provided by your employer. (To learn how much these programs pay, call the Social Security Administration, the Department of Veterans Affairs (VA), or your employee benefits office.)

After you complete the worksheet, combine your total immediate expenses with your total net cash flow to see how wide a gap exists between your expenses and your income. This gap is what your life insurance should fill. Depending on your life situation, you will probably discover that this gap is larger than you thought it would be.

Some simple rules of thumb can give you an idea of how much life insurance you need. At the least, you probably need seven times your annual income; at the most, 10 times. Many people require at least $100,000 of coverage, and most need several hundred thousand dollars more if they truly want to cover all of the immediate and future expenses listed above and in Roadmap 5.2: Survivor's Worksheet.

What Road to Take: Types of Life Insurance

There are many different types of life insurance that can appropriately provide income replacement for your family.

Term insurance pays your family a stated amount (the insurance policy "face" amount) if your death occurs during a specified period of time (for example, the next 10 years). Term insurance is useful when the insurance need is short lived. For example, you only need to protect your children's college funding plans until the last of your children is about 22. If you live longer than that, your need for this insurance will disappear. Likewise, your mortgage will be paid off at some point and your need to provide for child care eventually ends.

Whole life or universal life insurance (also known as permanent insurance) pays your family the face amount no matter when your death occurs. Permanent insurance can be either fixed or variable. Permanent insurance is best used for those insurance needs that never go away. For example, permanent insurance should be used as funding to support your spouse through their lifetime.

From a purely investment perspective, life insurance is unique. The expected "return" on a life insurance policy is impossible to calculate in advance. If you die prematurely, the return to your family is immense. However, if you live a long and happy life, the numeric return may be minimal

—but the peace of mind from always knowing your family could live as you wanted them to is huge.

The earnings grow tax deferred during your lifetime (that is, you don't pay taxes on any earnings that are left to accumulate inside the policy) and the face amount of your life insurance passes income tax free to your heirs at your death. If you name a beneficiary other than your estate, the face amount of your life insurance policy passes directly to that beneficiary—avoiding the cost, delays, and potential publicity of the probate process.

Keeping in mind the calculations you did to determine how much insurance you need, let's consider the pros and cons of the four basic types of coverage: term, whole life, universal life, and variable life. The debates about which type is best will rage forever among insurance professionals. You must decide what is best for you based on how much coverage you need, how much premium you can afford, and whether you want insurance only for its death benefit or also for its savings potential. Term insurance merely pays off if you die; whole life, universal life, and variable life insurance are versions of cash-value insurance, which combines a death benefit and an investment fund.

Term Insurance. This type of insurance offers financial protection on your life for a specified and finite period of time, usually one, five, 10, or 20 years. The only way your term policy will pay out is if you die during this period. In this case, your beneficiaries will probably be offered a lump-sum payout or a series of annuity payments. When the period expires, you may have the option to renew the policy, though at a higher premium because you are older and statistically more likely to die. If your policy offers a guaranteed renewal feature, you do not have to take a medical test or otherwise prove insurability to continue coverage for another term. You can also buy term insurance that provides a convertibility feature, which allows you to convert some or all of the coverage into whole life insurance without a medical exam. If you stop paying premiums on a term policy, your coverage ceases.

You can purchase far more protection for your dollar with term insurance than you can with a cash-value policy. Term insurance is therefore ideal if you have a large insurance need for a specific period of time. For example, you might need coverage for the years before your children become self-supporting, which should be in their mid-20s.

The chief advantage of term insurance is that it is very inexpensive. Hundreds of companies offer term; therefore, the market is extremely competitive. You can obtain price quotes on term coverage through most insurance agents, many direct mail insurers, or quote services such as AccuQuote, BestQuote, Choice Quote, Esurance, QuickQuote, QuoteSmith, Selectquote, TermQuote, and others. Make sure that the policy you buy is not only low priced but also backed by a financially strong insurance company. Preferably, the carrier should have at least an A rating from two or three of the major ratings agencies.

If you decide to purchase term insurance, check whether your employer offers such coverage and, if so, how much. As part of their employee benefits package, many companies provide the equivalent of one year's salary, while others pay double your annual income. You may also be able to get a good deal by buying more group term through your employer's plan, though you should compare those premium prices carefully with premiums on policies that you can obtain on your own. In addition, if you change jobs you will likely lose that coverage, which is why it is important to own your own policy. You may also be able to obtain a good group term policy through a trade association, an alumni group, or another organization to which you belong.

The disadvantage of term insurance is that the premium rises over time. As mentioned earlier, your premium stays the same during the term of a policy but increases each time you renew. This is because your chance of dying becomes greater as you age, and the insurance company needs to collect a higher premium to offset the greater risk of having to pay a claim. Term premiums rise slowly while you are in your 30s and 40s but start to get much more expensive as you progress through your 50s and 60s. By the time you reach your 70s, term insurance is expensive.

Cash-Value Insurance. Instead of buying term insurance, which offers pure protection, you can choose to purchase one of the several varieties of cash-value insurance. All of these policies, which are called whole life, universal life, or variable life, add a tax-deferred savings feature to the insurance protection component of the policy.

Whole life insurance. Whole life insurance, often called straight life or permanent insurance by agents, is the opposite of term insurance. While term starts with low premiums that rise over time upon renewal and provides you with no investment reserves, whole life locks in one premium rate for life, part of which is invested for your benefit. However, whole life premiums are much more expensive than term premiums, particularly when you are in your 20s to 40s.

Whole life remains in force as long as you live and pay your premiums. The younger you are when you buy a whole life policy, the lower your life-long premium rate. The insurance company uses your premium dollars to cover three expenses: death claims, administrative costs, and investments. Most of your money ends up being invested in stocks, bonds, real estate, and other capital assets that can appreciate and produce income over time. The cash value that your whole life policy accumulates results from those investments that are paid in the form of policy dividends, minus death claims and administrative expenses. All whole life policies, however, make a minimum earnings guarantee, usually no more than 4 percent.

One advantage of all forms of cash-value insurance is that your investment dollars compound tax-deferred. If you ever cancel or surrender your whole life policy, you can withdraw in a lump sum whatever cash value has accumulated, and you will pay taxes only if your cash value and policy dividends exceed the total amount of premiums you paid during the life of the policy.

You have several other ways to use any accumulated cash value in a whole life policy:

1. You can borrow up to the full amount of your cash value. You must pay nondeductible interest that usually floats two or three percentage points above the prime rate, which is far better than the rate you would pay on a credit card. If you have an older policy, it may even offer a low fixed rate. If you die before the loan is repaid (and there is no requirement that the loan must be repaid), your loan balance plus any interest due will be deducted from the death benefit paid to your beneficiaries.
2. You can tap your cash value to pay some or all of your premiums if you have built up enough value in the policy.
3. Once you reach retirement age, you can convert your accumulated cash value into an annuity, which can pay you a guaranteed monthly income for life.

Insurance companies have invented numerous twists on traditional whole life plans. Mostly, they offer different ways of paying premiums. Some of the most frequently sold varieties include the following:

1. *Modified life* versions start with lower premiums when you are younger, then compensate by charging higher premiums when you are older. Your

cash value buildup occurs more slowly in such a policy than it does in a traditional whole life policy.

2. *Limited-payment life* allows you to pay premiums for a certain number of years, usually between seven and 20, then stop. Premiums will be higher in such a plan, but cash values will build faster as a result.

3. *Single-premium life* is paid in one lump sum up front. Such a premium usually costs thousands of dollars, but you need not make another payment for the rest of your life. You must be careful to avoid adverse tax consequences with single-premium life if you want to withdraw money from the policy under some circumstances.

4. *Universal life insurance.* This form of cash-value insurance offers much more flexibility than traditional whole life policies. Universal life policyholders can pay premiums at any time and in any amount, as long as certain minimum levels are met. Also, the amount of insurance protection can be increased or decreased somewhat to meet your current needs. In addition, you always can tell exactly how much of your premium dollar is allocated to insurance protection, administrative expenses, and savings. These figures are never clearly disclosed when you own a whole life policy. Unlike whole life premiums, which are invested in long-term bonds and mortgages, universal life premiums reflect the current short-term rates available in the money markets. Insurance companies set a rate of return for one year, then readjust the yield up or down, depending on the level of interest rates. However, universal life policies guarantee a minimum yield of about 2 percent to 4 percent. A final advantage of universal life therefore is that the returns you earn on your cash value will reflect a sharp upturn in interest rates far more quickly than the returns on a traditional whole life policy. However, if rates fall or remain depressed, you may have to settle for lower returns for many years.

5. *Variable life insurance.* If you are willing to take higher risks in search of juicier returns, variable life offers the option of investing your cash value in stock, bond, or money-market funds managed by the insurance company. As with other cash-value policies, these returns compound tax deferred until you withdraw your principal. A good fund manager operating in a bull market can easily provide double-digit gains and outperform a traditional whole-life portfolio. But markets do not always rise, and this year's hero can become next year's goat. You have the option of shifting your money among stocks, bonds, and cash vehicles,

but the chances of selling at just the right moment are remote. Your investment timing affects not only the appreciation or depreciation of your cash value in a variable life policy, the death benefit also could rise and fall based on investment performance. However, the death benefit will never drop below the original amount of insurance coverage for which you contracted. Because the stock, bond, and money-market funds within variable insurance policies are legally considered securities, the life insurance agent who sells you a policy must be a licensed registered representative of a broker-dealer. The agent must give you a prospectus, as with any mutual fund, and explain the risks and all of the costs, as well as the potential rewards of the plan. When choosing a variable life policy, study the long-term track record of the funds offered. It is very difficult and expensive to switch out of one variable contract and into another under the management of a new insurance company if performance starts to lag.

There are two other versions of variable life: scheduled premium variable life and flexible premium variable life. The scheduled variety fixes the amount and timing of premium payments. The flexible style allows you to adapt the amount and timing of premiums to your changing needs.

6. *Second-to-die insurance.* One of the trendiest new forms of cash-value insurance, called second-to-die or survivorship life, is usually acquired in the names of a husband and wife. The policy pays a death benefit, intended to cover estate taxes, upon the demise of the insured who survives longer. Survivorship life premiums can be invested in either traditional whole life vehicles or in universal or variable options. Because the policy is based on the joint life expectancy of both husband and wife and only pays on the second death, the premiums cost less than they would if you bought traditional cash value policies on both lives.

Before you obtain this kind of insurance, however, make sure that your estate taxes will be significant enough to warrant the coverage. Ask a financial planner or an estate lawyer if they can set up trusts to reduce your estate taxes so that you won't have to pay survivorship life premiums.

7. *Accelerated death benefit insurance.* A fairly recent development in life insurance is the introduction of policies that allow you, in particular cases, to access your death benefit while you are still living. These are

known as accelerated death benefit or living benefits policies. These policies usually will make payments while you are alive under three circumstances:

▶ If you need long-term care, either in a nursing home or at home.

▶ If you are struck by a catastrophic illness or disease that runs up enormous medical bills. The policy lists specific diseases and surgeries covered, most commonly heart attacks, strokes, life-threatening cancers, coronary-artery bypass surgeries, renal failures, paralyses, and major organ transplants.

▶ If you are diagnosed as terminally ill. If your doctor confirms in writing that you have only weeks or months to live, you can tap your death benefit. Remember, however, that if you withdraw part or all of your death benefit while you are still living, your beneficiaries receive less (or nothing) when you die.

Term vs. Cash-Value Insurance. When you understand the differences between term and the myriad forms of cash-value life insurance, you must decide which is best for you. Some people believe that you come out ahead if you buy the cheapest quality term policy you can find and invest the difference between the term premium and the premium that you would pay on cash-value insurance in stocks, bonds, and mutual funds of your choice. Indeed, if you actually follow through on this strategy and build a sizable portfolio on your own through a disciplined savings regimen, you probably would come out ahead. By the time you retire, you not only would have had the insurance coverage you needed at a low price, but you also would have avoided paying the high commission charges wrapped into a cash-value policy.

Proponents of cash-value insurance say that, as well intentioned as most people might be they do not, in fact, exercise the discipline to invest the difference between premiums every year for the long term. The higher premiums paid into a cash-value policy are therefore a form of forced savings. In addition, the cash value accumulates tax deferred, while your personal investments are subject to yearly taxation unless they occur within an Individual Retirement Account (IRA), a Keogh account, a salary reduction plan, or another tax-deferred plan. Furthermore, the investments made on your behalf by the insurance company are chosen by a full-time staff of investment professionals just like those of mutual funds. You may or may not be skilled at selecting investments that perform consistently well over time.

You do not have to opt for only term or only cash-value life insurance. Your best choice might be to put together a combined policy that gives you adequate protection from term but also builds investment reserves from cash-value insurance. If your salary rises over time and you feel you can afford it, convert some of the term into cash-value insurance.

Annuities. In addition to term and cash-value life insurance, insurance companies sell annuities. Although annuities are issued by life insurance companies, they work quite differently than cash-value or term insurance policies. Annuities pay a regular stream of income while you live, usually after you retire, in contrast to life insurance, which pays your beneficiaries a lump sum when you die. Annuities also provide the advantage of tax-deferred compounding on the investment portion of the account.

There are two basic kinds of annuities: immediate and deferred. Immediate annuities are purchased with a lump sum (and begin to generate an income stream immediately). Typically they are purchased by people in retirement to provide a guaranteed stream of income. The lump sum might come from a distribution by a pension plan, a salary reduction plan, an IRA, a Keogh plan, or investments that you have built up over the years. Different insurance companies offer varying levels of monthly income, depending on how long you will receive payments.

Deferred annuities are bought by younger people who want to save tax deferred for many years, then convert to a payout schedule once they retire. You can purchase a flexible premium retirement annuity through regular monthly or annual deposits of as little as $25. You are not required to pay a premium every year, but the more you invest, the greater your annuity's value grows. You can also buy an annuity with one lump sum. This is called a Single-Premium Deferred Annuity (SPDA). Most companies require at least $2,500, though they prefer $10,000 or more. Annuities also have a life insurance component because your beneficiaries receive the entire accumulated value of your annuity (what you paid in plus the interest earned) if you die before receiving annuity payments.

If your life insurance policy accumulates enough cash value, you can convert that value into an annuity to boost your income stream in retirement. Take this step, however, only if your children are self-supporting and you no longer need as much life insurance.

Fixed vs. variable annuities. You have two annuity options. The more conservative route is a fixed annuity, which the insurance company invests in bonds or mortgages. Each year, the company announces the fixed return for the next year, depending on the current investment portfolio. The fixed return is the rate the company will credit to your annuity. The insurance company provides some level of guaranteed minimum return, however —usually 2 to 4 percent. Do not be lured by some company that offers a high first-year rate, which often drops dramatically in subsequent years. To protect yourself, make sure that your policy offers a bail-out provision. This gives you the right to liquidate all or part of your annuity without cost if your renewal rate is ever less than 1 percent of the previously offered rate. Usually, you must notify the insurance company within 30 days of receiving notice of the renewal rate that you plan to bail out. Nevertheless, do not rely on the bail-out clause if you opt for a fixed annuity. Choose a company that has paid a consistently above-average return, has below-average expenses, and has a rating of A or better by the major life insurance rating agencies. Chances are that its record will continue.

Your other option is a variable annuity, which offers the potential for higher returns, though at greater risk. The variable annuity contract gives you a choice among several stock, bond, and money-market portfolios. Within the stock category, you will normally be offered a selection of sector, aggressive growth, growth, growth and income, international, and balanced funds. With bonds, you may shift among corporate, government, high-yield, and international fixed-income portfolios. You can allocate your money among stock and bond options any way you like and transfer the funds as market conditions change. As the stock and bond markets swing in value over the years, your annuity's value also rises and falls. If you select a company with a proven investment performance, you can probably do far better in the long term with a variable annuity than with a fixed dollar annuity. The key is to purchase a contract with good numbers and a variety of top-notch investment managers. Because it is difficult and expensive to switch from one company's variable annuity to another's, it is worthwhile to research your decision carefully.

Payout options. Once you reach retirement age, annuities offer many different payout options. In general, the longer you obligate the company to pay benefits, the lower your monthly check. Whether you think that you will live a short or a long time determines your regular stipend. Each company determines its payout scale by estimating survival rates and the company's expected earnings on investments. The duration of annuity payments can be based on a life contingency, a period of time, or on a combination of the two. The following are the choices typically offered:

▶ *A 10-year term certain annuity.* If you think that you will live 10 years or less after retirement, you can choose an annuity that will pay you or your heirs for only 10 years. This option provides the highest monthly benefit. However, if you live more than 10 years, you're out of luck (at least as far as the company's obligation goes). This is a very risky strategy—unless you are in very poor health when you retire—because the average life expectancy today is well into a person's 80s, or more than 20 years from the usual retirement age of 65, and is increasing rapidly.

▶ *Life annuity with 10-year term certain.* This annuity will pay a fixed monthly amount for the rest of your life. However, if you die before the annuity has paid you benefits for 10 years, your beneficiary (usually your spouse), will receive your payments only for the remainder of the original 10 years. This form of annuity pays less than the 10-year term certain. It also is significantly risky for your spouse, who would not receive payments after 10 years from the date of your retirement, assuming that you have died. If you select this option, make sure that your spouse has enough other sources of income to fall back on to cover the shortfall.

▶ *Life annuity.* This plan would cut your monthly payout from the 10-year term certain significantly but would assure you of an income for life. After you die, your beneficiary receives no payments.

▶ *Joint and survivor annuity.* If you are married or if someone depends on your income, you may want to select this option, which pays a fixed amount until both you and your spouse or dependent die. When you die, your spouse or dependent receives Qualified Joint and Survivor Annuity (QJSA) payments until they die. These payments are usually less than the amount you received, but by law they cannot be less than 50 percent of your payment. Because both you and your spouse or dependent may live a long time, the joint and survivor plan offers the lowest monthly payment of those options discussed here. However, it is also the safest plan because it ensures that your spouse or dependent will receive a monthly income after you are gone.

If you are married and want to receive your benefits on the life annuity option or assign your survivor benefit to someone other than your spouse, you must obtain written spousal consent confirming that your spouse knows what they are relinquishing and are doing so willingly. (If you are asked to sign such a consent form, don't unless you fully understand the financial impact of the alternate election and are so wealthy that you can't envision ever needing the money.) Once you start receiving payouts from annuities, you must pay ordinary income tax on a portion or all of those payouts. Each payment is considered part investment earnings and part return of your original principal unless it came out of a qualified plan. You must pay tax on the investment earnings but not on the return of capital. The insurance company informs you how much of each payment constitutes earnings and principal. Unless you absolutely need access to your annuity money before retirement, don't touch it. If you take distributions from your annuity before age 59½, you not only must pay income tax on the earnings but you also owe the IRS a stiff 10 percent early withdrawal penalty. The only ways around this penalty before age 59½ are if you suffer a disability or if you die and the annuity proceeds are distributed to your beneficiaries.

Annuity fees and expenses. Pay careful attention to the many fees attached to every annuity contract. Most companies do not explicitly charge an up-front commission, or load. Instead, they levy a hefty surrender charge of as much as 10 percent of your principal if you want to transfer your annuity to another company within the first five to 10 years of the contract. After that time, the surrender charges may disappear. However, many annuities offer a free withdrawal provision after the first year and for every year thereafter that surrender charges apply. This allows the contract holder to withdraw a certain percent (usually up to 10 percent) of the accumulated account value. (Prior to age 59½, these partial withdrawals would be subject to penalty tax as well as income tax.)

In addition, most annuity marketers charge annual maintenance fees of $25 to $50 to cover the administrative costs of maintaining an account. For variable annuity contracts, annual asset management fees of ½ percent to 2 percent are also assessed, just as they are in regular stock and bond mutual funds. Another significant fee that applies only to annuities is the mortality and expense fee, which typically ranges from 0.6 to 1.4 percent. All of these fees are deducted automatically from your investment account. Most annuity charges do not apply to immediate annuities because once you have purchased such a contract, you cannot surrender the contract. Therefore, they do not directly impose maintenance or asset management fees. The fees, if applicable, are netted out from the monthly payments you receive.

Bumpy Road: Sales Charges and Other Expenses

Whichever type of life insurance policy or annuity contract you choose, be particularly wary of high fees and expenses. Some insurers pay their salespeople much higher commissions than others, and you can be sure that those sales charges will come out of your pocket one way or another. Sales commissions usually are not stated explicitly in an insurance contract, but they are most often paid out of your first few years of premiums. High commissions might hit you in the form of slower cash value buildup, reduced dividends, or greater expenses. One way to get around such high fees is to buy from one of the growing number of low-load insurance carriers that sell mostly over the Internet, phone, and through the mail.

Whenever you purchase a policy, determine the cancellation fees or surrender charges for pulling out of the contract. These fees can be quite high, such as 7 percent of your accumulated cash value, particularly if you want to withdraw in the first few years of your policy. Think long and hard about switching from your current policy to a new one, despite any strong encouragement you receive from an agent. It takes years for your cash value to accumulate significantly, and you can lose a good deal to fees if you transfer to another policy.

Comparing Costs. When you have narrowed your search for the best policy to a few companies, you can use the interest-adjusted net cost index to help you make your final decision. This index, available for both term and cash value policies, factors in all financial elements of an insurance policy, such as the company's dividend record, expenses, premium costs, and timing of payments. The result allows you to compare the price of policies, all things being equal. The index is expressed as a cost per $1,000 of insurance. For example, a policy with a $5 cost index costs $5 per $1,000 of coverage per year, or $500 for a $100,000 policy. These index costs range from a low of about $1 to as much as $10. Ask your agent for this cost index on two or more comparable policies, though they might not volunteer the data eagerly. The lower the cost index, the more insurance your money buys. Another objective source from which to obtain this data is the latest issue of *Consumer Reports* that examined life insurance.

While you size up the insurer, the insurer also evaluates you as a potential risk. On the insurance application form, it asks your family medical history, occupation, age, sex, and health habits (such as smoking or drinking), as well as other factors that affect your chances of living a long time. The insurer may even ask you to undergo a medical exam from a doctor of the company's choosing. Once it compiles your profile, the insurance company rates you a preferred, standard, or substandard risk. Preferred risks have the least likelihood of dying prematurely and therefore pay the lowest rates. Standard risks are a bit more likely to die early because of health problems and therefore pay higher rates than preferred risks. Substandard risks smoke, drink, are overweight, and have a history of medical problems in their families. As a result, they pay high rates for coverage.

Air, Sea, or Land Route: Choosing a Life Insurance Company

Because life insurance is a long-term commitment, you want to make sure that the company you choose will be around years from now to fulfill its part of the bargain. Therefore, examine a company's financial strength ratings as published by A.M. Best, Standard & Poor's, Moody's, Duff & Phelps, and Weiss Research (each have Web sites), or your local library may be able to help.

Also, evaluate the service you receive from the company's representatives. The agent should go over the insurance contract with you carefully before you sign so that you understand its key clauses. After you buy your policy, you probably will not have much contact with your agent, but the person should be able to answer questions knowledgeably and readily.

Using Your Computer to Buy Insurance. The computer can save you a substantial amount of money in the insurance buying process in three ways: analyzing your needs, educating yourself about insurance, and finding the cheapest policy. By using software that is part of broader-based personal finance packages like Quicken or Microsoft Money, or online calculators that are the feature of many insurance-oriented Web sites, you can make an accurate assessment of how much insurance you really need. That is the first step to saving money, because such an analysis makes sure you don't buy too much coverage and waste money in excess premiums, or too little, exposing yourself to significant financial risk.

There is also a wealth of information online to teach you everything you wanted to know about all forms of insurance. The Internet can also be a powerful tool for searching for the least expensive insurance policy. The art of locating the best policy is most highly refined in the term life insurance market, because term is a simple product that is relatively simple to compare based on price. There are many insurance quote services with Web sites that allow you to get quotes instantly, based on your health condition and how much insurance you need. Other Web sites specialize in specific product lines, such as annuities.

The emergence of computers and Web sites is revolutionizing the process of buying insurance. No longer do you need to be the captive of whatever your local insurance agent tells you. By exploring some of the Web sites listed here, you can probably find a much better deal, saving yourself hundreds or thousands of dollars while increasing your coverage.

Mom and Dad,

As you know, we'd always struggled with finances, making every dollar count, as most young couples with an 18-month old do. I miss Toby terribly, but you don't have to worry about us financially. When Toby died, I became responsible for the largest sum of money that I ever imagined would cross my path.

Toby left us with plenty of money to set aside a trust for our son and plenty of time for it to grow. I can't tell you how proud and relieved I am knowing that there's college money and enough to provide a nest egg for Steven to start his adult life.

I feel immense pressure to be wise with the money left to me; at times I am overwhelmed by the responsibility. Toby and I worked so hard to make ends meet, I feel a little guilty because now my ends meet, but he isn't here to enjoy it.

But I also know how lucky we are that Toby insisted that we plan our estate, set up a trust for Steven through his will, and bought some life insurance to help us do it all!

Love to you both,

Patty

No one ever said buying insurance was going to be much fun. Picking your way through the complexities of life insurance is a chore you probably want to postpone indefinitely. But don't. Once you go through the process of obtaining the proper kind and amount of coverage, you will have earned a benefit that is hard to put a price on: peace of mind.

Cruise Control: Protecting Your Business

A complete discussion of business insurance is beyond the scope of this book. However, if you own a business, there are several reasons to consider insurance.

1. Insurance can protect a business from economic loss when the business loses key knowledge, skills, experience, funding, or contacts as the result of an important employee's death or disability. This is referred to as "key person" insurance. That "employee" could be you. How does your family receive the value of your business if you are the key employee and you are gone? Life insurance is the only reasonable and certain way.

2. In a sole proprietorship, partnership, or closely held corporation, business continuation following the death or disability of an owner is critical to the surviving owners and employees. In many cases, the business has to be liquidated to settle the estate of the deceased owner. Buy/sell agreements, funded by life insurance on the life of the owners, allow the surviving owners (or employees) to buy out the deceased owners' interest without liquidating the company and to maintain the business as an ongoing concern.

3. Life insurance can be used for credit enhancement. Generally, banks will be willing to loan more, at better terms, if they know the business is indemnified for the loss of a key person and are assured that the business can continue in the event of the death of the owner.

Life insurance can also be used in a business situation to fund special employee benefits, such as nonqualified deferred compensation and split-dollar plans.

Traveler's Checks: Cash When You Need It

While life insurance is only a piece of the estate planning process (as Chapters 3 and 4 demonstrate, trusts and gifting strategies also play a huge role), it is an important piece.

Life insurance can be used to pay estate and inheritance taxes, and because life insurance provides cash at exactly the time when estate and inheritance taxes need to be paid, having life insurance designated for this purpose can mean that your family doesn't have to sell off other assets (like the family home or business) to pay the taxes. Typically, life insurance purchased for this need is held in an irrevocable life insurance trust.

The other key use for life insurance in your estate plan is to substantially increase gifts to loved ones or charities. Life insurance leverages your bequest assets. A relatively small premium can fund a large life insurance face amount that can be used to provide gifts, at your death, to anyone you want —including favorite charities, your spouse and children, other relatives, key employees, and special friends.

So many people look at the expense of life insurance and think, "This could never happen to me." But what if it did? Do you want your family to suffer unnecessarily because of your failure to plan?

► Family Package: Social Security Benefits

This is not the place to discuss the gamut of benefits currently provided under the federal government's Social Security program, but it is important to note that it will also provide regular income to your family if you die, no matter how old you are or whether you have accumulated enough work credit hours. Not everyone is entitled to survivor's benefits, however. Family members can collect if they are a(an)

- ► widow or widower at least 60 years old;
- ► widow or widower at least 50 years old who is disabled;
- ► widow or widower of any age who cares for a child who is 16 or younger
- ► or a disabled child receiving Social Security benefits;
- ► unmarried child younger than age 18;
- ► unmarried child younger than age 19 who is enrolled in an elementary or secondary school full-time;
- ► unmarried child 18 years or older who has a severe disability that started before the child reached age 22;
- ► parent who depended on the deceased for at least half their income;
- ► ex-spouse who is at least 60 years old (or 50 years old and disabled) and was married to the deceased for at least 10 years before the divorce; or

▶ ex-spouse of any age if they still care for a child eligible for benefits on the deceased's record.

A family's survivors' benefits can total between 75 and 100 percent of the basic Social Security retirement benefit, depending on several factors. However, survivors can receive no more than between 150 and 180 percent of the basic monthly benefit. If the combined benefits from all family members exceed that amount, the total survivors' benefit will be reduced proportionately. Amounts are constantly changing, so consult your local Social Security office or visit their Web site at http://www.socialsecurity.gov.

▶ Optional Tours: Pensions, IRAs, and Other Benefits

No matter how much Social Security you qualify for, as a sole source of income, it is clearly not enough to maintain a comfortable standard of living. If you have planned well, you will have a regular source of pension income to enhance your retirement lifestyle. But what happens to those benefits when you die?

Extra Mileage: Pensions

Many public and private employees are provided pensions through their jobs. Some pensions are entirely financed by the employer; others are co-financed by the employer and the employee.

Currently, many employers offer 401(k) retirement plans that defer taxes on both employer and employee contributions and earnings until funds are withdrawn from the plan, usually at retirement. (Tax penalties apply to early withdrawals, except in certain circumstances.)

Many people, even if they are covered by a pension through their employment, have established Individual Retirement Accounts (IRAs), often in addition to their 401(k) plans. The law allows a person who is under age 70½ and over age 50 and who has earned income to deposit up to $5,000; those under age 50 may contribute up to $4,000 (this amount can change, so check with the IRS, your financial advisor, or accountant), or the amount of one's earnings (whichever is smaller), into a traditional IRA account each year. Spousal IRAs, generally set up on behalf of a non-working spouse, are also available. Contributions to an IRA may be wholly or partially tax deductible, or nondeductible (depending on whether covered by a qualified pension plan, such as a 401(k), filing status, and modified adjusted gross income level). IRAs defer taxes on earnings from contributions until the funds are withdrawn, usually at retirement. (Again, tax penalties apply to early withdrawals, except in certain circumstances.)

Several other tax-deferred plans, accounts, etc., can also help an individual to defer taxes until, theoretically, they have reached an age where their earnings have begun to decline. For example, self-employed individuals may establish a Keogh plan which allows for larger, tax-deferred yearly contributions and greater benefits than does an IRA. Another tax-deferred retirement option for self-employed people is a simplified employee pension plan or SEP, which is a type of IRA.

Many more types of pension or retirement plans are available—savings plans, segregated asset account plans, annuity plans, and so on. Regardless of the type of retirement plans you are participating in, it is critical that your heirs are aware of those plans. At your death, one or more of those plans may provide dependency payments to your spouse and/or minor children, or may provide a substantial pay-off to a designated beneficiary or to your estate. On the other hand, a plan may provide nothing at all.

Types of Plans. As mentioned, there are two forms of pensions: one your employer provides without any contribution from you, and one to which you contribute part of your earnings during your working years, either through your employer or through a separate plan, such as an IRA or a Keogh account. In the best of all worlds, you would qualify for both types of pensions.

For those employees who qualify, defined benefit plans can provide a substantial portion—from 10 to 40 percent—of your total retirement income. The amount you receive often depends on how many years you worked for your employer and your salary in your final few years at the company.

As a rule, as long as you are vested in a defined benefit plan, your spouse will receive pension benefits if you die. Ask your benefits department how much your spouse might get in survivors coverage if you were to die before retirement. Usually, the benefit is half the amount you would have received had you retired, and it is paid starting in the year you would have stopped working, usually age 65. This is known as a pre-retirement survivor's annuity. If your spouse signs a document waiving the right to this annuity, you will earn a larger pension benefit when you retire. However, when you die, your surviving spouse will not receive a pension from the company. In general, we

Hazard!

Pension Maximization—Or, Is It?

Many insurance agents recommend a straight life annuity payout option (often called pension maximization) instead of the joint and survivor option. While straight life pays a higher monthly amount, payments cease once you die. Insurance salespeople advocate taking a portion of the higher payments and buying an insurance policy to provide capital to cover your spouse's needs once you die. While this strategy may sound good in theory, it usually is not in practice. The cost of the insurance policy can consume most or all of the extra income and the size of the death benefit may not adequately support your spouse for the rest of his or her life.

don't recommend taking this option. Consult a qualified financial advisor or pension expert to discuss the pros and cons of all of your options.

If your employer does not offer a traditional defined benefit pension plan, it probably offers a defined contribution plan, such as a 401(k) which gives you the opportunity to put aside money from your salary on a tax-deferred basis. Unlike a benefit plan, a contribution plan does not obligate your company to pay a certain pension benefit. Instead, you may set aside a certain contribution, which your employer may or may not match. Either way, however, you must choose among various investment options. This decision makes you responsible for the ultimate size of your pension benefit. Like income from all other pension plans, investment earnings from defined contribution plans grow tax deferred. However, that deferral ends upon your death when your heirs take distributions.

The money in a defined benefits plan pays to your beneficiaries upon your death prior to retirement. It is part of your estate and should be treated as part of your estate and decisions about how and to whom to leave it should be assessed in the context of all other assets. You don't necessarily need a complex trust agreement, and you don't necessarily need to hire a lawyer. You just choose the person to whom you want the money to go. When you die, the assets in your 401(k) become the property of the beneficiary you named in the official beneficiary documents you filed with the financial institution handling your account.

Traveling with IRA

Although traditional IRAs offer a lot of tax benefits while you're alive, they can trigger some tax and other complications after you die. That's why it's important to plan ahead, so that you can avoid—or at least reduce—the impact for you and your beneficiaries.

If any money is left in your IRA when you die, who gets it? As with 401(k)s and similar plans, that's up to you. What your will says doesn't matter. In fact, it doesn't matter if you have no will. The beneficiary you select is a kind of "will substitute." In other words, your IRA generally doesn't have to go through the probate process. The assets in your IRA, however, will pass automatically to your beneficiary, under the terms of the IRA contract in much the same way that a life insurance policy's death benefit goes directly to the beneficiary upon the policyholder's death. With an IRA, beneficiaries can avoid the potential delays, expense, and publicity that can accompany the probate process in some states.

Watch for Potholes: Give Your Plans a Regular Check-Up

As we've seen, with any defined contribution plan, whether employer provided or an IRA, you can name whomever you wish as your beneficiary. It doesn't have to be your spouse. It doesn't have to be a relative. The point is that you get to choose. With that freedom comes responsibility.

Changing Beneficiaries. Some plan owners repeatedly change their wills but forget to file beneficiary forms. This can be a big mistake. So don't forget about your plan; it may be your single biggest asset. Be sure to name not just a primary beneficiary, but also a contingent beneficiary, sometimes called a successor beneficiary. This person can inherit the funds if the primary beneficiary dies before you do.

There are important practical and financial reasons for taking these steps. For example, if you fail to name a beneficiary, odds are that the money will become part of your probate estate and will have to be processed through a probate court. (This will also happen if you name your estate as the beneficiary.) This can result in unwelcome fees and other consequences.

Keep in mind that you may change your beneficiary selection even after you turn 70½.

This option may be especially important if you want to stretch out the life of plan as long as possible, so that the account not only generates a steady stream of income for you and your beneficiaries over time, but also has a chance to grow.

If you have multiple beneficiaries, you may want to establish separate IRAs while you're alive, naming a separate beneficiary (and contingent beneficiary) for each. This may make things more convenient for the beneficiaries after your death: each beneficiary can choose, separately, what to do with an IRA. One may want to withdraw all of the money, another may want to withdraw in several annual installments, and another may want to stretch out withdrawals over a lifetime.

If you're married and have more than one beneficiary, creating separate IRAs while you're alive can also be convenient and helpful to each beneficiary after your death. For example, if your spouse is the sole beneficiary on one of your IRAs, your spouse may get to roll over the IRA and treat it as their own, postponing withdrawals until age 70½ for traditional IRAs, without regard to what the other beneficiaries do with their accounts (they may want to commence withdrawals sooner, for example). So, even if you don't create separate accounts while you're alive, your beneficiaries have the right to do it by December 31 of the year that follows the date of your death.

Alternate Route: Using a Trust. Although you can name your own beneficiaries for your IRA, and your IRA can pass directly to them after you die, in some instances it may be better to name a trust to receive your assets instead.

If you want your assets to pass to children who are minors, for example, a trust can ensure that the assets are properly managed until the children are old enough to make decisions for themselves. (The trust can make payments to the person who oversees a custodial account for the minor.)

In fact, if you use a trust and name the right people as trustees, you can have some comfort knowing that the assets you've accumulated inside your IRA will be properly managed for all of your beneficiaries—whether they're minors or adults. When you die, the financial institution that serves as the custodian or trustee of your IRA can distribute funds to the trust, which in turn can issue payments over time to the trust's beneficiaries.

If the trust is set up correctly, the payments to a trust beneficiary can be stretched out over the life expectancy of that beneficiary. In other words, the payments needn't be made in a lump sum or paid out within five years, so the

Hazard!

Know the Law

If you live in a state with community property or marital property laws—Arizona, California, Idaho, Louisiana, Nevada, New Mexico, Texas, Washington, or Wisconsin—you may have to get your spouse's consent before you name, or add, a beneficiary who is not your spouse. Check with your IRA trustee or custodian—and your lawyer—to see how the laws of these states may affect your beneficiary decision.

tax impact of each payment is reduced and more money remains to grow on a tax-deferred basis. In other words, if you name a trust as the beneficiary of your IRA, it can be treated, in effect, as an individual, allowing withdrawals to be stretched out over a longer period of time. That's because, under certain circumstances, you can "look through" the trust to use, as your designated beneficiary, the names of one or more people who are beneficiaries of the trust. You (or your legal advisor) must make sure, however, that the trust meets all of the rules to qualify for this special treatment.

Using a trust also gives the trustees the flexibility to speed up payments if the beneficiary needs more money. Another advantage involves protection from creditors, although creditor protection for IRAs varies from state to state. For example, some states shield IRAs from the claims of creditors; other states have restrictions. If your IRA holds a substantial amount of assets, a trust may be able to shield those assets from creditor claims against your beneficiaries after you die. In weighing these and other potential benefits of a trust, you must also consider the legal and other costs associated with creating and maintaining the trust.

If you think a trust may suit your needs, consult a lawyer who is familiar not only with trust rules, but also with how trusts interact with IRAs. This is not a do-it-yourself matter; you need professional legal advice.

The Stretch IRA. A Stretch IRA isn't new; in fact, technically, there's no such thing in federal tax law as a stretch IRA. It is simply a strategy to take full advantage of the existing rules so that you may stretch your IRA over the longest possible period of time. As a result, the IRA can benefit not only you but also your beneficiaries—and their beneficiaries, too.

The stretch IRA concept essentially assumes that you'll take only the minimum required withdrawals from your IRA while you're alive, and that your beneficiaries will do the same. All the while, the investments inside the account will generate handsome returns. As a result, the IRA will not only generate a steady stream of income for you and your beneficiaries, but will also build up a potentially huge reserve of wealth, to be passed from generation to generation.

Here's the key. Because only the minimum amount is withdrawn each year, more money can remain in the account. Because the account can survive for decades, the investments inside it can grow and grow, all on a tax-deferred basis—and it's perfectly legal.

The possibility of stretching your IRA over generations—providing income for beneficiaries and building wealth inside the account all the while—makes IRAs an increasingly appealing place to park your retirement savings.

This is especially so if you've built up wealth in your retirement savings plan at work, in a 401(k), 403(b), 457 governmental plan, or other such arrangement, since you may in many instances move your money from the plan you have at work to an IRA. If you want to employ the stretch-out strategy, an IRA may be the only place to be; your employer-sponsored plan simply may not give you this chance. A word of caution: Before you transfer money from an employer-sponsored plan, check the rules or you could be subject to taxes and other restrictions. With proper planning, this strategy can work to your advantage.

Beware of Sales Pitches. Many financial advisors are well aware of the potential benefits of this strategy and can help you take the steps you'll need to take full advantage. Just be careful. In their sales materials regarding the stretch IRA strategy, some advisors use unrealistic assumptions in an attempt to lure your business.

Remember that financial advisors may benefit by having your IRA under their umbrella. That IRA can generate a steady stream of annual income for them, too, in the form of various commissions, management fees, and expenses. There's nothing fundamentally wrong with that, of course; everybody needs to get paid for the services. However, some people and products cost substantially more than others. Look for the best, lowest total cost provider.

However, when considering where best to place your IRA and how a stretch IRA strategy may benefit you, you should first take a careful look not only at the fees and other expenses a financial advisor may charge, but also at the underlying motivations the advisor uses to attract your business.

For example, while the stretch IRA strategy may well prove helpful to you and your beneficiaries, it may not generate the enormous wealth that some financial advisors or institutions imply they will. In some cases, sales presentations for stretch IRAs give hypothetical examples showing how much the IRA will generate in income over the years and, more important, how much value can be built up inside the IRA over that time—sometimes for periods of up to 90 years. Remember, however, that such huge dollar values depend on a lot of assumptions, and those assumptions may not be practical.

If the sales presentations you review don't make sense for someone in your circumstances, ask the salesperson to use more realistic assumptions. After the salesperson changes the figures based on assumptions that you feel are more realistic, check whether the new projected results make sense to you and are in line with your goals.

Even if the representative of a financial institution knows all about the stretch IRA strategy and how to put it to work for you, the financial institution that stands behind the advisor may have roadblocks in place that could cripple this strategy after you die (overly restrictive beneficiary forms, for example).

For these and other reasons, enlisting the help of a lawyer, accountant, or other trusted advisor who is familiar with the rules and how they may apply to you is a good idea.

The advisor can request that a financial institution adapt its policies to your needs, or can draw up a customized beneficiary form that you and the financial institution find acceptable. By taking these and other steps, the advisor can help ensure that your stretch-out strategy is not only implemented but also maintained after you die.

Estate Taxes. Although your IRA will bypass probate court when you die, it may not escape federal estate taxes. If your estate is large enough, the assets in your estate—including your IRAs—will be subject to the federal estate tax. The balances in your IRAs will be added to your estate for purposes of figuring any estate tax that's due.

That's not necessarily something to worry about. Most taxpayers don't have enough in assets even to have to think about the estate tax. However, if the value of your estate exceeds the threshold, you can reduce it.

Planning for Liquidity. If you've got the bulk of your assets tied up in IRAs or other retirement savings plans, you'll also have to make sure the rest of your estate has enough in liquid assets—cash or assets that could be quickly converted to cash—so that sufficient funds will be available to cover tax, legal, administration, funeral, and other expenses that will come due at your death. (Your lawyer, planner, accountant, or other advisor will also help you plan for any estate or inheritance taxes your state may levy.)

Keep in mind, too, that your beneficiary must also be prepared to pay some income tax, either immediately upon inheriting your account or some years down the road because, unlike some other assets, IRAs and other retirement savings plans don't enjoy a stepped-up in cost basis upon the owner's death, as do stocks, mutual funds, and other such assets.

No Basis with IRAs, 401(k)s, 403(b)s. If you have a traditional deductible IRA, 401(k), etc., there is no tax basis in your account. So the entire value of the account, including your original contributions plus any earnings, will be subject to tax, either when you withdraw the money or when your beneficiary withdraws money after you die.

If you have a traditional nondeductible IRA, your account will have a basis for tax purposes, equal to the amount of after-tax dollars you contributed. But when you die, that basis will be carried over to your beneficiary; it won't be stepped up to the value of the account at your death. So, if a wife contributed $5,000 in after-tax dollars to a traditional nondeductible IRA, and the account is worth $85,000 at her death, her spouse beneficiary will have a carryover basis of $5,000. He won't have to pay income tax on the original $5,000 in contributions, but he will have to pay tax on any earnings the account has generated over the years. As a result, if he withdrew the entire $85,000 after the wife's death, he'd have to pay federal and probably state income tax on $80,000.

This is an important point to keep in mind for your estate-planning purposes. The deductible contributions and all earnings in your traditional IRA will be taxed at some point, either when you withdraw it or when your beneficiary does. So while IRAs offer some tax benefits during your "wealth-accumulation years"—either through tax deductions for your contributions, tax deferral on your account earnings, or both—any withdrawals made by you, or by your beneficiary after you die, won't be eligible for favorable capital gains tax treatment.

They'll be taxed as ordinary income. It's also possible that the assets in your IRA could be taxed twice, according to two different tax systems. If your estate is large enough, your IRA could be subject to the federal estate tax, and the person who inherits your IRA may eventually have to pay federal income tax on any withdrawals (although the beneficiary may be eligible for a special tax break in such a situation).

It's vital to keep in mind that, if your IRA is your chief asset, your beneficiary may be forced to make withdrawals—and suffer income tax consequences—if no other cash is available to pay funeral and burial expenses, legal bills, final medical costs, and any other expenses that may typically arise as a result of your death—including the federal estate tax (and any state tax that may be triggered).

For these and other reasons, it's a good idea for you to get expert help to put together a sound estate plan that can resolve thorny tax, legal, and other issues in advance of your death. Make sure, too, that your plan includes enough liquidity—enough cash or assets that can be converted quickly to cash—to cover expenses so that the IRA won't have to be tapped to pay these costs.

If your IRA is your chief asset and it's big enough so that estate tax will be triggered, consider establishing an irrevocable life insurance trust. If the trust is properly arranged, the proceeds from the policy can be used to pay the estate tax, leaving the IRA intact.

Using Your Exemption. Here's another estate-planning strategy you should consider. If you die and have enough assets to trigger the estate tax, remember that a portion of your estate can escape the tax altogether. With careful advance planning, you can choose which of your assets will qualify under this exemption. Your IRA? Your stocks? Your mutual funds? The point to remember here is that, with a little advance planning, you can reduce the impact of estate and other taxes on your heirs. Just make sure you hire a qualified lawyer (and other financial advisors) to get the job done.

Gifts to Charity. If you're inclined to give a portion of your estate to charity, consider donating your IRA instead of other assets in your estate, such as stock, since your beneficiaries won't qualify for the stepped-up basis on an inherited IRA. In addition, each dollar your beneficiaries withdraw from a traditional deductible IRA will be subject to federal and possibly state income tax, at their highest applicable rate; donating an IRA to charity may reduce the amount of taxes your heirs have to pay.

This is particularly true since your beneficiaries will be eligible to claim a stepped-up basis on stock or other securities they inherit outside of a retirement plan. This benefit is especially valuable if the stock has appreciated in value over the years. If you give the IRA to charity and the stock to your beneficiaries at your death, they'll get the stepped-up basis, and the profit they realize when they eventually sell the stock will be taxed at more favorable capital gains rates.

Join the Army and See the World: Veterans Benefits

The Department of Veterans Affairs (VA) is charged with administering benefits available to persons who have served on active duty in the U.S. military service. The benefits depend upon the veteran's length of service, the era during which the service was performed, whether the veteran is disabled, and whether the disability was caused by active service, among other things.

Under certain circumstances, the following benefits (and many more) may be available to a veteran:

- ▶ Pensions for disability caused by service-connected injury or disease
- ▶ Pensions for certain non-service-connected disabilities
- ▶ Hospitalization benefits
- ▶ Nursing home care
- ▶ Outpatient medical treatment
- ▶ Insurance

Certain benefits are available to your heirs if you were separated from the service under conditions other than dishonorable.

1. *Burial flag.* An American flag may be issued to drape the casket of an eligible veteran. After the funeral service, the flag may be given to the next of kin or close friend or associate of the deceased. Flags are issued at any VA office and most local post offices.
2. *Burial in national cemeteries.* Any deceased veteran of wartime or peacetime service whose last period of active service terminated other than dishonorably may be buried in a national cemetery. In addition, the spouse, surviving spouse, or minor children of an eligible veteran may be buried in a national cemetery. In each instance, space must be available. There is no charge for a grave or for its opening and closing.

3. *Transportation of deceased veteran to a national cemetery.* The VA may pay the cost of transportation of a deceased veteran for burial in a national cemetery if the veteran died of a service-connected disability or the veteran was receiving disability compensation from the VA.

4. *Headstones or markers.* The VA will furnish, upon request, a headstone or marker to be placed at the unmarked grave of a veteran whose last discharge was other than dishonorable. This service is provided for eligible veterans whether they are buried in a national cemetery or elsewhere. A headstone or marker is automatically furnished if the burial is in a national cemetery. Otherwise, application must be made to the VA. The VA will ship the headstone or marker, without charge, to the person or firm designated on the application.

5. *Reimbursement of burial expenses.* The VA is authorized to pay an allowance toward the funeral and burial expenses of an eligible veteran. A veteran not buried in a national cemetery will be paid an additional allowance for a plot for interment. If the veteran's death is service-connected or if the veteran died in a VA hospital, the VA is authorized to pay a larger sum for the burial and funeral expenses.

6. *Dependency and Indemnity Compensation (DIC).* DIC payments may be authorized for widows or widowers, unmarried children, and low-income parents of service personnel who die during active duty as well as veterans whose deaths were service-connected (when death occurred on or after January 1, 1957). The exact amount of the basic benefit is determined by the military pay grade of the deceased veteran. Payments are also made for children between age 18 and 23 attending school.

7. *Non-service connected death pension.* Surviving spouses and unmarried children under age 18 (or until age 23 if attending an approved course of study) may be eligible for a pension if their income does not exceed certain limits.

8. *Education for spouses, widows, widowers, sons, and daughters.* If a veteran is completely disabled or dies as a result of service, the VA will generally (but with some exceptions) pay to help educate the widow or widower, and each child beyond the secondary school level, including college, graduate school, technical and vocational schools, apprenticeships, and on-the-job training programs. Education loans are also available.

If you are a veteran, your heirs should seek assistance through the Department of Veterans Affairs in order to apply for available benefits. For more comprehensive information about veterans benefits, request a copy of the Federal Benefits Manual for Veterans and Dependents from your local VA office.

Traffic Accident: Workers' Compensation

Workers' compensation laws have been adopted by all the states. Although their details vary greatly, the general purpose of workers' compensation programs is to provide income to workers who are unable to work as a result of an injury or occupational disease arising out of the worker's employment. While incapacitated, they receive a monetary benefit based on their average wage and number of dependents. In addition, medical expenses related to the injury are paid by the employer or the employer's insurance company.

Here, however, we are primarily interested in workers' compensation benefits available to dependents of a deceased employee. Ordinarily, the spouse and minor children of an employee who died as the result of a work-incurred accident or occupational disease are entitled to weekly payments for a certain period. Usually, the spouse is entitled to payments for a specified number of years or until remarriage, whichever is sooner; and the dependent children are entitled to benefits until they reach a certain age.

Ordinarily, the laws also provide that the widowed spouse, or the deceased employee's estate, is entitled to a specific funeral or death benefit. It is important that your heirs be made aware of any life-threatening injuries or occupational diseases you incurred during the course of your employment. If your death is subsequently caused by such an injury or occupational disease, your dependents may be entitled to substantial monetary benefits.

Paving the Way

Planning for Your Family's Future

▶ Traveling with Young Children

Parents of minor children face special issues and concerns and need to make a lot of decisions while planning their estates.

Hiring a Guide: Caring for Minor Children

Doing an estate plan is especially important for people with young children. Until your children turn 18, one of the greatest responsibilities you have toward them is deciding who will take care of them if you are no longer alive. If you do not take the steps necessary to appoint a guardian, your children can wind up under the guardianship of someone you would have never trusted with your child.

Most states have a priority system that determines who is entitled to become the guardian of your children. Generally, the surviving parent has priority, even if they are not the custodial parent. After the surviving parent, typically the grandparents have priority, followed by the children's aunts and uncles. If you do not want your parents or your spouse's parents to raise your children, you need to do something about it.

Knowing that you need to select a guardian is one thing; actually making the selection is another. It is hard to imagine anyone else raising your children, but it is even harder imagining the wrong person raising your children. There are a few important things on which to focus when deciding on a guardian for your children:

▶ The guardian only needs to be responsible for your children through the age of majority (age 18, in most states). If you were ruling out people because of age (for example, the grandparents), you may want to reconsider.

▶ If you are thinking of a couple (for example, your sister and brother-in-law), is it really both people you intend to name? What if your sister predeceases you? Do you really want your brother-in-law as guardian? Or, do you only want your children raised by a married couple and not by either person individually?

▶ Who is your choice as secondary guardian? It may have been difficult to choose an initial guardian, but you should always have a second choice just in case your first choice is unable or unwilling to carry out that responsibility.

▶ If your children are in school, does your guardian live in the same area, so that your children do not have to change schools? If not, would your guardian be willing and able to move so as not to further disrupt your children's lives?

▶ Does your guardian share your same thoughts about religion, education, or responsibility? Sometimes people focus only on family members as guardians, even though there may be others who are more closely aligned with their beliefs on child rearing. Your guardian will, after all, be the one raising your children.

▶ Does your guardian have a good relationship with your family and with your spouse's family? If not, will the guardian encourage relationships and visits with those family members?

▶ Are there additional messages you want to leave for your guardians or for the people you didn't name as guardian? For example, maybe you want to give the reasons why you made your selection. Or maybe you want to encourage your guardian to move into your home. You may want to make sure that the guardian understands that visits with "crazy" Uncle Joe should be supervised.

Also, keep in mind the consequences of making guardianship contingent on certain specified events. Suppose that you name your sister as guardian of your four-year-old and six-year-old but only on the condition that she never moves the children from their home. What if 10 years later, with the whole-hearted approval of the children, your sister takes a new job requiring her to move to another city? Are you really going to have the children removed from her care at that point? If you have particular desires, state them but try not to make them a condition of guardianship. Otherwise, your children who have lost their parents might also be taken away from their guardian. Just think through the consequences.

Naming a Personal Guardian. Depending on the state in which you live, the only way you can legally designate a personal guardian for your children— the person who would raise your children should both you and your spouse die—is through your will. As we said, it's wise to also designate an alternate personal guardian.

You can name two people as co-guardians for your minor children, which may make sense if the co-guardians are married or in a committed, unmarried relationship. However, in a society where an estimated 50 percent of all marriages fail, there could be problems if the co-guardians divorce or their unmarried partnership ends.

Note: If you have more than one young child, you can name a different guardian for each child or one guardian for all of your children. Which arrangement makes the most sense depends on your family's situation.

After your death, a court must confirm the appointment of your children's guardian, a process that is usually completed without a hitch unless someone comes forward to contest the appointment. If there are problems, a hearing will be held to determine what is in the best interest of your children.

If you die without naming a legal guardian for your minor children, it is possible that a family member or close friend may begin raising your children, acting as a de facto guardian (guardian in fact). This may not present any problems until the guardian tries to add your children to the family's health insurance policy, enroll the children in school, arrange surgery for your children, or take some other action on behalf of your children that requires the consent of a parent or legal guardian. At that point, the de facto guardian would have to initiate a legal process to become your children's legal guardian. The court may name the de facto guardian legal guardian, or it may decide to appoint an adult family member, close friend, or someone

Hazard!

Protecting Your Choice

▶ If you have reason to expect that your children's legal guardianship may be contested, it's a good idea to leave money in your will to help pay for an attorney to fight the contest.

▶ In some states, you can use your will to stipulate whom you do not want to serve as your child's guardian in addition to whom you do want.

else. It is possible that the person who becomes your children's legal guardian may be someone you don't like or who doesn't share your values or your attitudes toward children rearing.

Qualities to Look for in a Personal Guardian. It goes without saying that the person you choose as personal guardian for your children should be someone of good character whom you trust to do a responsible and caring job of raising your children. That person should also share your basic values and be willing to respect any special wishes you may have regarding how you want your children brought up. Obviously, your children's personal guardian should not have a drug or alcohol problem or a history of emotional problems. Most important, however, that person should have the time and the interest in taking on the role of guardian.

If your children are old enough to have opinions about who they would like to have as a guardian, ask them unless you think that having the conversation would be too upsetting. Listen carefully if a child raises serious objections to a potential guardian.

If You Are Divorced or Separated. If you are divorced or separated and have custody of your children, by law, when you die, your ex-spouse (the children's biological or legal parent) would get full legal responsibility for the children. Should that parent then die, assuming your ex-spouse wrote a will, whomever your ex named would raise your children.

If you don't want your ex to raise your children, you can say so in your will and name the person you would prefer to have that responsibility. However, because your reasons for making this request are probably not flattering to your ex, it's usually not a good idea to state them in your will. If you do, your ex-spouse may sue your estate for libel. Instead, provide your executor with a written statement of your reasons, and, if you have any records or other documents that support your request, attach copies of them to the statement. If you take this route, be sure to talk with your executor or beneficiary to explain why you want the contest, and if you have the resources, leave money in your will for your executor or one of your beneficiaries to pursue a contest of guardianship should your ex-spouse decide to raise your children despite your wishes.

Despite your will, a judge would probably award child custody to your ex-spouse, the child's only remaining legal or biological parent, unless your ex does not want that responsibility or unless the court decides that your ex is an unfit parent. Ongoing problems with drugs or alcohol, a criminal record, a history of serious mental illness, or a failure to be actively involved in your children's life for a long time, among other things, could induce a judge to make that determination.

Future Travel Plans: Providing for Minor Children

Your options for transferring assets to minor children include:

1. Leaving money and other property to your spouse or to another adult with the express understanding that they be used for your children's benefit.
2. Using your will to leave money and other property to your minor children.
3. Naming your children as beneficiaries of your insurance policy, employee benefits plan, or IRA.
4. Leaving money and other property to your minor children through the Uniform Gifts to Minors Acts (UGMA) or the Uniform Transfers to Minors Act (UTMA), discussed in Chapter 3.
5. Setting up a trust for your children.

You may decide to use just one of these options or a combination of them to transfer your assets to your children. Their advantages and disadvantages are outlined in Roadmap 6.1.

The law in every state assumes that minor children do not have the knowledge or the maturity necessary to make wise decisions about substantial amounts of money and other assets and therefore need an adult to manage those assets for them. In addition, children do not have the legal

Roadmap 6.1

Options for Transferring Property to a Minor Child

Option	Advantages	Disadvantages
1. Leave money and other property in your will to your spouse or another for the benefit of your child	▶ No need for a property guardian ▶ Involves no extra expense or paperwork	▶ No guarantee that your child will actually benefit from the money and other property ▶ Assumes that spouse or other is a good financial manager
2. Leave money and other property to your minor child in your will	▶ Involves no extra expense or paperwork	▶ Goes through probate ▶ Depending on value of what you leave your child, you must appoint a property guardian ▶ Your child will receive money and other property at age 18 or 21, depending on your state
3. Name your child as beneficiary of your life insurance policy, employee benefits plan, IRA	▶ Avoids probate ▶ Involves no extra expense or paperwork	▶ Depending on value of death benefits, you must appoint a property guardian ▶ Your child will have full control of benefits at age 18 or 21, depending on your state
4. Use the UGMA or UTMA	▶ Custodial accounts are easy to use and relatively inexpensive to set up ▶ Account custodian, not property guardian, manages assets	▶ Irrevocable ▶ In most states, your child will take control of money and other assets at age 18 or 21, depending on your state ▶ You must set up a separate account for each child
5. Set up a trust for your child	▶ Offers maximum flexibility and control over disbursement of trust income and when child takes control of trust assets ▶ Trustee manages assets in trust	▶ Relatively expensive to set up ▶ Depending on type of trust, can be time-consuming to set up

right to enter into contracts or to buy and sell real estate, stocks, bonds, and other property—actions that may be necessary depending on the types of assets you leave them. Therefore, although the dollar maximum varies by state, if you use your will to leave a child more than $2,500 to $5,000 worth of assets, you need to name a property guardian for your child in your will. This person will manage the assets on your child's behalf if you die while the child is still a minor.

Route 1: Leave Assets to an Adult for Your Minor Child's Benefit

An extremely simple option for leaving property to minor children is to leave it to your spouse or to another adult in your will, stipulating that the property must be used for your children's benefit. You can even spell out the specific things you want the assets to be used for—funding your children's college education, for example.

This option has a few minor advantages: (1) You don't have to name a property guardian for your children because you are leaving the assets to your spouse or another adult, not directly to your children. (2) This option does not involve any additional expense or extra legal paperwork. Furthermore, the adult to whom you leave the assets is not legally obligated to maintain any records or report to the court regarding the assets.

On the other hand, this option presents some important potential disadvantages, especially if the value of the property you've earmarked for your minor children is substantial: (1) It gives you absolutely no control over how the assets will be managed or even whether they will be used for your children's benefit (despite what you state in your will). (2) It also assumes that the adult you leave the property to will never be tempted to use the assets for their own benefit. (3) If the adult you leave the assets to dies without a will while your children are still minors, you have no guarantee that your children will receive the assets you intended for them.

Route 2: Leave Assets to Your Minor Child through Your Will

Including your minor children in your will offers some of the same advantages as the previous route; namely, no extra paperwork or expense. However, this option has some potentially significant drawbacks.

1. If the value of the property you leave your children exceeds the dollar maximum your state stipulates that young children can legally own

without adult supervision, you must use your will to designate a property guardian to manage those assets on behalf of your children. Some states require that property guardians put up a bond, and all states require that they make periodic reports to the court. To comply with this requirement, the property guardian may need to hire an attorney or a CPA, the cost of which will come out of the property you leave your children.

2. Your state will require the property guardian to take a very conservative approach to the management of those assets. Therefore, the guardian may not be able to maximize their value. On the plus side, however, that requirement prevents the property guardian from jeopardizing your children's assets by putting them in high-risk investments.

3. Your children will get full control of the assets you leave them in your will when they become legal adults. Yet your children may not be mature enough or financially savvy enough to manage them responsibly, especially if their value is substantial or the assets are relatively complex.

Route 3: Naming Your Child as Beneficiary of Your Life Insurance Policy, Employee Benefits Plan, or IRA

Another way to provide financially for your children in the event of your death is to make them the beneficiaries of your insurance policy, employee benefits plan, or IRA. At your death, the proceeds from these assets—the death benefits—will automatically pass directly to your children, avoiding probate and the claims of creditors.

Depending on the value of the benefits, you must appoint an adult to manage them for your children until they become legal adults; the benefits will not be released otherwise. If you arrange to have the benefits paid directly to your children, the adult you appoint to manage the benefits will be a property guardian. If the benefits are placed in a trust, the adult will be a trustee; and if the benefits are deposited in a custodial account under the Uniform Gifts to Minors Act or the Uniform Transfers to Minors Act, the adult in charge of those assets will be an account custodian.

Route 4: Using the UGMA or UTMA

Leaving assets to minor children using the UGMA or the UTMA is simple and inexpensive (see Chapter 3). Low cost and ease of setup are not the only advantages of custodial accounts. Another is that account custodians don't deal with the state oversight and control that property guardians have to contend with. Therefore, they can do more to maximize the value of the assets in a custodial account and increase the income they may generate.

UGMA and UTMA accounts come with some potential disadvantages, too: One is that in most states your children get full control of the assets in the account as soon as they become legal adults, regardless of whether they are emotionally and financially prepared to manage them. In some states you can extend a custodianship until your child turns 25.

A second minor drawback is that you cannot set up one custodial account for multiple children. To leave assets to more than one child, you must set up an account for each. Also, any income or gain earned by the assets in a custodial account must be reported to the IRS in your child's name as your child is the account's legal owner. If your child is younger than 14, the child will be taxed at the parent's tax rate. However, when your child turns 14, the tax rate will be at the child's tax rate.

A final disadvantage is that the assets you place in a custodial account are treated as inter vivos gifts. Therefore, if the total of the assets transferred into an account in a given year exceeds your annual $11,000 per person gift limit, you must file a federal gift tax return, and the excess will decrease your total federal estate tax exemption.

Account Custodians: You can name yourself custodian of your child's UGMA or UTMA account, or you can appoint someone else, your spouse, another relative, or a friend. Don't forget to designate a successor custodian as well.

Account custodians are entitled to receive a fee for their services, although a relative or close friend is apt to waive the fee.

Account custodians are not subject to the state scrutiny and control that property guardians have to deal with. They are free to manage the account assets as they see fit and disburse income from an account as needed, and they have no reporting requirements to comply with.

Route 5: Setting Up a Trust for Your Minor Child

A trust is an excellent estate planning tool for transferring a substantial amount of property to minor children. Flexibility and control over the terms of the transfer are the primary benefits of a trust. The control is a particular advantage if you are leaving your children a considerable amount of money or if the assets you are transferring to them are particularly complex. Another important benefit of a trust is that you can give the trustee considerable independence and control over the management of the assets in the trust and the dispersal of any income they generate (see Chapter 4 for detailed information about various types of trusts).

Frequently, when parents set up a trust for a minor child, one parent names the other as trustee. With this arrangement, a minor child's property guardian is often the logical choice for alternate trustee because both jobs require someone who is comfortable dealing with money and investments. Another option is to name the property guardian as primary trustee and someone else as alternate.

Route 6: Leaving Property to Adopted Children

No matter what their ages, your adopted children have the same inheritance rights as your biological children in most states. But if you want to be absolutely certain that they do, you have two options when you write your will. You can specifically designate each of the children you are leaving your property to or you can state that you are leaving your property to "all of my children" and then define exactly what you mean by that phrase, being sure to include your adopted children in the definition.

Special Needs: Providing for a Child with Disabilities

There are several things to consider when planning for the care of a disabled child (whether minor or adult) after your death. In all probability, you will want to

- ▶ set up a trust to hold the assets that you'll leave,
- ▶ provide for a successor guardian in the event that your child will require one, and
- ▶ leave a document that describes your child, their condition, and your hopes and expectations so that those you trust to care for your child have some guidance.

Guardianship. If your child is an adult who requires a guardian, then you already may have had the court appoint you as guardian. If so, you most likely will not be able to designate an alternate or standby guardian in your will (as you could for a minor child). Designating an alternate or standby guardian must be done in court, during your lifetime. If you have not already taken steps to name an alternate or standby guardian, you should do so.

Letter of Intent. Although not a legal document, a letter of intent is important because it provides the courts, your child's future caregivers (should they be required), and the trustee, if any, with valuable information on what you would prefer for your child and what you expect of them. If you don't have one, write one, ideally with your child.

Trust. Before setting up a trust, you need to answer two major questions to determine whether you should. Will your child eventually need Social Security disability or Medicaid services? If the answer is yes, then most likely you will want to create a special needs trust. If the answer is no, ask yourself the next question: Will your child be able to make financial decisions on their own? If yes, then no special planning is necessary. Leave your estate as you would to any other child. If you believe that the disability may reduce your child's earning capability, you may want to leave a greater portion of your estate to the disabled child than to your other children. If your child will not be able to make financial decisions, then a standard trust could be set up. The trustee would be responsible for making financial decisions for the child.

What is a Special Needs Trust? If your child depends on Medicaid or Social Security disability, or will in the future, a special needs trust can provide for your child without endangering those benefits. A special needs trust does, however, require that the trustee be someone other than the beneficiary. A special needs trust specifically limits what the trust is allowed to pay for in such a way that the beneficiary still qualifies for Medicaid or other government services. The trust can hold an unlimited amount of funds and can own a house or a car, or other items, which would otherwise disqualify a person from government benefits.

A note of caution: The wrong language in the trust documents can invalidate it. Then the entire fund will have to be used to pay for needed services before the beneficiary will again qualify for covered services. It's critically important to consult a lawyer with specific experience in drafting a special needs trust.

Choosing a trustee. It is important to make this decision as a family. Parents often believe that their non-disabled children will take care of their disabled sibling after the parents die. Or, conversely, they do not wish to burden their non-disabled children with the care of their disabled sibling. Your children may, however, surprise you. Once you have talked as a family, consider carefully who should be the trustee.

A corporate trustee, like a bank trust department, offers certain benefits. The corporation will be long-lived. While bank trust officers may come and go, the bank or its successor carries on. A corporate trustee often provides professional money management, bookkeeping, and tax preparation. A corporate trustee will also charge a fee and, more than likely, the bank or trust department's staff will not know your child or your child's unique needs.

A family trustee, on the other hand, often will work for free and know your child and their specific needs. Family members may, however, have to pay service providers to handle investments, provide bookkeeping, and file taxes. Another serious consideration is how being in charge of the purse strings will affect the family member's relationship with your child. Will the relationship survive if potentially inappropriate requests are denied? When selecting a trustee, be sure to think through the personal dynamics.

Remember, too, it's possible to have both family and corporate co-trustees. While difficulties may arise if trustees disagree, the benefits could outweigh the difficulties. It also may be possible to assign individual trustees designated areas of responsibility in the trust agreement.

Group Travel: Blended Families

Blended families are increasingly common today. Estate planning for blended families is more complex than for traditional families for a variety of reasons: You may have more money saved, and your children and new family members may have competing interests in your property. Still, now that you are remarried, you may want to leave all of your estate to your surviving spouse. If you do that through your will and you have children from a previous marriage, you have no guarantee that your spouse will plan the estate so that at least some of those assets will go to your children, especially if your spouse has children from a former marriage. If your spouse and your children do not get along, you may have real cause for concern.

To prevent potential conflicts:

1. Consider a prenuptial or postnuptial agreement. A legally binding prenuptial agreement is a contract written and signed before the marriage that spells out the rights, obligations, and duties that each of you will have during the marriage. A postnuptial does the same thing, except it's created after you are married. They are an especially good idea if you have substantial assets or children to protect. The goal is to identify what as-

sets and liabilities each partner brings to the marriage and to determine how those assets brought into the marriage and those acquired during the marriage will be divided, if necessary. The agreement can spell out exactly how each of you will divide up your estates after your deaths, including what you will leave to your children.

2. Review how your assets are titled. Any property you and your new spouse acquire after getting married can be owned as joint tenants with right of survivorship (see Chapter 3). This allows property to pass directly to the surviving spouse should one of you die. You also should look at your current life insurance policies and retirement accounts (like a 401(k) or an IRA) to update your beneficiaries. If you want to name a person(s) other than your new spouse as the primary beneficiary(s) of your qualified retirement plan assets, you need your spouse's written permission to do so.

3. Update your wills and trusts. Be sure to update your will so it clearly spells out your goals. It is also a good idea to make sure that everyone concerned knows your wishes. If your children feel slighted, they might challenge your will after your death. Also, if you want your stepchildren (who may have no legal rights to your estate) to inherit from you, use your will to spell out your wishes for them. Coordinate the provisions of your wills to provide for one another and for any children either of you has from a previous marriage. Because either of you can change or revoke your wills at any time, however, you run the risk that your spouse's will could be changed, leaving nothing to your children.

   Trusts can be useful in dictating how you want your assets disposed of. You can attach strings to how your money is used and managed. For example, you might want a trust to make sure your children eventually inherit your home but that allows your current spouse to live in it during their lifetime. Your attorney can help you set up a trust that would provide for your surviving spouse and then transfer the trust assets to your children after your spouse dies.

4. Consider your children's needs vs. your new spouse's needs. Typically, most of your assets pass to your spouse when you die. This is equally true when you remarry. In a traditional family, that's not a problem, and the family assets typically pass to the children after both parents are gone. When you remarry, however, you probably want to provide for your spouse as well as your children from your previous marriage. To

avoid a "yours, mine, and ours" situation, it's important to be proactive at the outset. If you are not, problems like the following can arise:

▶ When you're dead and your spouse is retired, they might want safer, income producing investments. Your children, however, may want growth of principal so something is left for them when they inherit.

▶ Your children may watch every penny that your spouse spends. How will they feel if your surviving spouse wants to buy a new car?

▶ If your new spouse is much younger than you, your children may have to wait a long time before they inherit what remains of your estate.

Here are some possible solutions.

▶ Put together a plan that effectively disconnects the money left for your spouse from the money left to your children. You will, of course, want to consult an attorney or estate planning professional to ensure that your plan is structured properly.

▶ Life insurance can be an effective way of making sure that your children receive money when you die instead of having to wait until both you and your spouse have passed away. Your children can be the primary beneficiaries of your life insurance policies.

▶ Another option is to have your children take out a life insurance policy on you that makes them the owners and beneficiaries of the policy and you the insured. You can gift them money each year, and they in turn can use that money to pay the premiums. Or you can establish an irrevocable trust to hold the life insurance for their benefit. This approach is useful if you have minor children.

Handing Over the Wheel: Leaving Property to Adult Children

You can transfer property to your adult children using any of the estate planning tools you might use to transfer property to any other adult beneficiary. Depending on your family situation, however, you may want to address special issues related to your adult children in your estate planning. For example, if some of your children are much better off financially than others, or if some of them have children and others don't, you may want to leave some of your children more than others. Also, if one of your children is a poor money manager and you plan on leaving them a substantial amount of assets, you may want to be sure that your child does not squander the inheritance. One way to do that is to set up a spendthrift trust (see Chapter 4).

Fork in the Road: Leaving Property to Out-of-Wedlock Children

In most states, if you're a woman and your will says that you are leaving property to "all of my children," that term includes any children you may have had outside of marriage. On the other hand, if you're a man, that definition usually includes only the children born to you and your wife as well as to any children who have proved that you are their biological father. Regardless of your sex and your state of residence, however, you can explicitly include or exclude your out-of-wedlock children when you write your will. If you have any out-of-wedlock children, it is advisable to consult with an attorney about the inheritance laws of your state.

Exit Ramp: Disinheriting a Child

Nearly all states have laws regarding pretermitted children, or children left out of a will. These laws say that a child who is not included in the parent's will is legally entitled to an intestate share of that parent's estate unless the will makes clear that the parent intended not to include the child. The laws vary as to the circumstances under which these laws apply, and how much a pretermitted child is legally entitled to inherit varies from state to state. For example, some laws apply only to children born or adopted after a will is executed, while others apply to all children regardless of when they were born.

If you want to disinherit one of your children, talk with an estate planning attorney. They can explain what your state's law says about disinheritance and help you write your will so that your wishes will be carried out. You should also explain your reasons for the disinheritance to the executor of your estate, and, depending on the circumstances, you may also want to talk with the child you are disinheriting so that your action does not come as a painful surprise after your death.

Simply not mentioning one of your children in your will is no guarantee that the child will actually be disinherited. Also, you risk opening the door to a will contest after you die. For example, the child you left out of your will could argue that it was an oversight and that you didn't really intend to disinherit them. If your will was contested, depending on the laws of your state, a court would probably award the child some portion of your estate. How much would depend on such factors as whether your spouse was still living and how many other children you have.

▶ Adventure Travel: Your Business and Your Estate

Private company ownership has long been a path to wealth. Owners of small businesses (with fewer than 500 employees) represent about 20 percent of the $20 trillion in private wealth in the United States according to a recent study by Oxford Information Technology Ltd.

The benefits of private company ownership range from freedom to set one's own compensation to rapid decision making, risk-taking, and the opportunity to enjoy the fruits of hard work. For some, it is the ability to realize a dream, to create a successful business, and to see it grow and evolve. For those who inherited or continued a business started in an earlier generation, it is the opportunity to take a company to a new level, to grow a business from an existing foundation, or to put one's own stamp on it. For others, it is the ability to keep family assets in one operating business as a way to protect future generations as well as a way to create a legacy (i.e., building something bigger than oneself that lasts beyond one's lifetime).

Therefore, if you are a business owner, you have special estate planning issues to consider. Answering the following questions can help you determine which issues you face, which will in part depend on the legal structure of your business, and how best to deal with them.

1. What do you want to happen to your business after you die? Your options include sell it, pass it on to one or more of your family members to own and run, or liquidate the assets.
2. If you want your business to continue as a source of income for your beneficiaries, who will own it and who will manage it?
3. How will you transfer ownership of your business to the new owners?
4. Do you have a succession plan in place?
5. What is the value of your business? How should its value be determined?
6. Do you want your business to go through probate? If not, what can you do to protect it from that process?

7. How will your estate taxes be paid? If you are like many people, your business is your most valuable asset, but without appropriate tax planning, your family could be forced to sell your business or liquidate its assets to pay your estate taxes (see below for details).

8. If you want your business sold or liquidated after you die, what should you do now to prepare for that transaction?

If you are a business owner, hire an estate planning attorney who has specific experience working with businesses.

Public Transportation vs. Private Car: Your Business' Legal Structure and Estate Planning

If your business is a sole proprietorship, you may be its only employee. Therefore, when you die, your business will probably die too, for its viability is totally dependent on your skills, knowledge, and business contacts.

You have several options regarding the future of your sole proprietorship when you do your estate planning. One option is to find someone to take over your business. That person could be one of your children, your spouse, a friend, another business owner, or even a stranger. If your business has substantial assets and if its client list is valuable, another option is to sell the business. A third option, if your business owns substantial assets that would be of value to someone else, is to arrange for the liquidation or sale of your business assets after you die.

When your business is a partnership, you share its ownership with one or more partners. Therefore, you can't decide by yourself what will happen to your share of the business after you die or how much your share is worth. Those are decisions you must share with your partners. In fact, they may be addressed in the partnership agreement you drew up when you established the business.

If your business is incorporated and you do not own 100 percent of the corporation's shares, what will happen to those shares when you die and what they are worth are not up to you. A buy-sell agreement or shareholders' agreement should address those issues. They can establish an up-front value for your shares and provide an automatic market for those shares.

Who's Going on the Next Vacation? Succession Planning

If you want your business to continue as a growing concern after you die and it is a sole proprietorship or a family-owned business, then as part of your estate planning you must identify your successor. Your successor could be a family member, an employee, or someone else.

A written plan helps ensure a smooth transition from yourself to your successor. The plan should address the future management and ownership of your business, the roles and responsibilities of the future owner, and other relevant financial and legal business issues.

> *Hire an estate planning attorney with expertise in business matters to help you develop an ironclad succession plan.*

Here are some of the issues to consider prior to preparing your plan:

1. Who will have primary decision-making responsibility for the business?
2. How will any profits your business earns be divided up? For example, if you want your children to take over your business, do you want the children who will be most actively involved in running it to get the greater share of its profits, or do you want each of them to get the same share?
3. Should some family members have voting stock and others have nonvoting stock?
4. If your business is sold after you die, do you want your beneficiaries to have ongoing roles in the business? If so, what should these roles be?
5. How should the sale of your business be structured?

If you want your business to continue after you die, and if you are relying on it to provide either short- or long-term income to your family, it's a good idea to identify your successor while you're still actively involved in the business. That way, you can provide that person with the training and on-the-job experience needed to fill your shoes. This will give you an opportunity to assess whether the person really has what it takes to fill your shoes and your successor can make sure that they really want the job. If either of you has second thoughts about the planned succession, you can select a new successor.

If you choose one of your children as your successor and your business is a closely held corporation in which you own 100 percent of the shares, you must decide whether to leave the entire business to that child or just a majority interest. If you choose the first option, to be fair you may want to give your other children assets that are equal in value to the value of your business or structure some other financial arrangement that benefits them as much as you benefit the child who inherits your business. You face the same fairness issue if one of your children takes over your sole proprietorship or your share of a partnership.

Once you have decided what you want to have happen to your business after your death, openly discuss your wishes with your family. You want to be sure that everyone understands and is comfortable with your plans. Otherwise, you risk the possibility that family discord may surface after your death, which could jeopardize the stability of your business.

Hazard!
Don't Do It Yourself

One entrepreneurial trap is to think that the responsibility for choosing the successor is entirely up to you. That thinking is changing. Today, as in public companies, a private company's board—if there is one—should be involved in all aspects of succession planning. Meanwhile, you should nurture a succession culture so that promising executives are given jobs intended to broaden their skills.

If you don't have a board, don't forget your family—bring them into the decision-making process.

Transferring Ownership

If you want to leave your share of your family-owned partnership or corporation to your children or spouse after your death so that it can continue operating and generating income for them, you must decide how best to transfer ownership. One option, if your business is incorporated, is to give your family members shares of stock, possibly as annual inter vivos gifts. This approach also reduces the size of your estate for tax purposes.

Another option is to take advantage of the unlimited marital tax deduction by leaving your business or your share of the business to your spouse. Although this approach provides your estate with tax benefits, it can create future estate tax problems for your spouse. Your spouse faces the same potential problem if your business is a sole proprietorship. (You can learn more about the unlimited marital tax deduction in Chapter 3.)

Another option is to leave the family member who will own your business enough money to purchase all of its stock. One way to provide the funds for that purchase is to buy a life insurance policy and name that future owner as beneficiary.

Liquidating Your Business Assets

If there is no one in your life that you want to succeed you as owner of your business, if you don't want your business to continue after your death, or if it is unlikely that your business will be able to continue because your knowledge and/or skills are integral to its success, your best option may be to liquidate it. Liquidating a business involves selling its assets.

To prepare for a liquidation, develop an inventory of your business assets, including your accounts receivable. Describe and provide a current value for each asset. Update the inventory on a regular basis to ensure that it remains an accurate reflection of your business assets over time. Keep the inventory with your will.

You may want to include with your inventory a list of reputable business liquidators, including their names, addresses, and phone numbers, so your family will not have to develop that information themselves after your death.

Estate Taxes

If you want your business to continue after you die so that it generates income for your family and if you believe that your estate will be liable for taxes, it is critical that you determine how those estate taxes will be paid. Otherwise, your family may be forced to sell your business or to sell key assets owned by your business to pay the taxes.

An estate planning attorney can help you determine how your business fits into your estate planning and what you can do to minimize your estate taxes and protect your business. Here are some strategies you may want to consider:

1. If your business is a corporation, reduce the value of your taxable estate by giving away up to $11,000 worth of your company's stock each year to each of your children or to others ($22,000 a year if you and your spouse both make the gifts).
2. Take advantage of the unlimited marital deduction by leaving your business to your surviving spouse. If you use this deduction, however, you may be creating potential tax problems for your spouse. One way to deal with this potential problem is to place some or all of your business in a bypass trust and make your spouse the beneficiary of the trust.
3. Sell your business to your children or to someone else while you're alive. Be aware, however, that you will have to pay taxes on the profit you realize from the sale.
4. Establish a Grantor-Retained Annuity Trust (GRAT) if your business is closely held. This irrevocable trust provides your estate with federal tax benefits and also pays you a fixed amount of money for a specified period of time. When that time is up, the assets in the trust—company stock or other income-producing assets—transfer to the trust beneficiary.

Minimizing Estate Taxes with Gifts of Partnership and LLC Interests. For estate tax purposes, your heirs are not taxed on items that are not in your estate. You can use the annual gift exemptions to help accomplish this goal. However, making gifts presents two major challenges:

1. Large assets, such as a family business and real estate, are difficult to transfer in small parts.
2. You lose control of the asset once it is gifted.

The limited partnership and LLC help solve both of these challenges in that they permit you to divide an asset into pieces. For example, a parcel of real estate can be transferred in parts, but this would require a new deed each year to transfer a small percentage of the property. If the property were transferred into an LLC, the yearly gift can be accomplished by a transfer of an interest in the LLC, not the real estate itself. Second, you can retain control of the asset by remaining a general partner, or in the case of an LLC, the manager. If properly structured, you can give as much as 99 percent of

Hazard!

Making Young Children Partners in Your Business

If you make your minor children partners in your business, you will need to establish a custodianship or trust to hold the interest for the benefit of the children. This technique should not be attempted without the assistance of a qualified attorney.

your limited partnership or LLC interests to your heirs, yet still remain in full control of the assets of the partnership or LLC.

Limited partners generally have no right to demand distributions of income, participate in management, or force a liquidation of the partnership. Similarly, members of an LLC who are not managers cannot demand distributions of income, participate in management, or force a liquidation of the company. This lack of power results in a lack of value for the partnership or membership interest. That is, if a limited partner or member tried to sell their interest, no one in their right mind would pay full value for the interest, especially in the case of a family partnership. This lack of marketability for the partnership or LLC share is taken into consideration for estate tax purposes.

Furthermore, if the deceased parent's remaining interest is a minority share, there is an additional discount, because the interest lacks the controlling vote. The discount for a minority interest may be another 20 to 30 percent. Keep in mind, however, that while the minority-holding member is alive, the person may still have effective control by acting as the general partner or manager.

Leveraging Your Gifts. Because gifts up to $11,000 per year to any person are exempt from taxation, you can combine this strategy with the LLC or limited partnership for maximum effectiveness. A membership or partnership interest already has a reduced valuation (see discussion above), so an effective gift of as much as $22,000 per year can be made. In other words, a gift of partnership or membership interest that has a "book value" of $22,000 may be made with a discounted tax value of closer to $11,000. We recommend that you retain professional counsel before attempting to use this powerful technique.

Probate and Your Business

The probate process can inhibit efficient business decision making and damage your business in the process. Therefore, depending on how your business is structured, you may want to protect it from probate. One way to do that is to place your business in a living trust; another option is to own it as a joint tenant. Again, seek the advice of your estate planning attorney.

Avoiding Ancillary Probate. If you own property in other states, a proceeding, called "ancillary probate," must be completed in each state. Once you transfer your assets to a limited partnership or LLC, your interest is considered "intangible personal property." This type of property goes where you go. Thus, if all of your assets are held in partnerships or LLCs, your assets will become localized to where you reside, and ancillary probate is avoided.

Continuity of Business. A death in a family business can often lead to financial disaster. Without proper planning, a business can be wiped out because the estate is not liquid enough to pay its taxes. If you were to die without a will, a personal representative would be appointed by the court to oversee the business while your estate is resolved. Your assets are then in control of a court-appointed representative, not your heirs. The probate process could take months, even years to complete. In the meantime, the business could fall apart.

Establishing your business as an entity apart from you as its owner will prevent this kind of disruption. Generally, the death of a general partner of a limited partnership or member of an LLC will dissolve the business.

Hazard!

Warning on Family Partnerships

The IRS closely scrutinizes family partnerships, particularly the annual gift exclusion. You must be able to show that there was a completed gift. Retention of income, undue control over partnership assets, and forbidding your children from selling their shares may result in an incomplete gift. See your legal advisor before attempting any of these strategies.

However, most properly drafted agreements permit the surviving partners or members to continue the business. In addition, the assets of the business belong to the partnership or LLC, not to you as an individual. Your interest in the partnership or LLC becomes part of your estate. The personal representative appointed by the court is not in control of the business.

> *If you are a business owner, consider choosing an executor who has experience running your particular type of business.*

When you don't specify what happens to your possessions in your estate plan, it can lead to arguments among family members—or worse. Without giving your heirs some sort of direction, their conflicting claims are likely; in fact one of the most common sources of disagreements among heirs involves personal effects. It is not the big-ticket items—the house, brokerage accounts, and retirement plans—but the grandfather clock, mother's opal earrings, or the oil painting over the mantle that becomes the center of rifts among family members.

It is important to remember that when your intended beneficiaries are different from your natural beneficiaries, only a will or trust will ensure that the proper people inherit. Not every case results in litigation, but sometimes family members stop speaking to each other for years.

Part of the problem is that most people, even when they do put together an estate plan, leave personal effects "equally" to the children. Because it wouldn't be practical for each child to take one-third of the grandfather clock or split its use every four months, equal comes to mean equal in value. But value, when it comes to personal effects, rarely has anything to do with money. Dividing personal effects equally among the children could really turn out to be anything but equal. And, who makes the decision as to what is an equitable division?

There are several ways to go about planning for the distribution of personal effects. Here are a few of the more creative solutions we have come across:

1. Make a list of all of the items of value in your home and assign beneficiaries to each of them. If you spell out who gets what, you will minimize the chance of disagreements among your beneficiaries.

Dear Katie,

Pauline, Joanne, and I were all pretty close growing up. As we grew older, we got married and moved to different parts of the country. We keep in touch by phone and at family reunions every couple of years.

When Dad died, he left a handwritten will that left everything equally to the three of us. "Everything!" All that was left was about $14,500 equity in the house, $750 in the bank, a $10,000 life insurance policy. The cash was used to pay for the funeral and burial and some outstanding bills, which left only the items in the house.

That's where the problems began. It started innocently enough. Joanne mentioned that Mom told her she could have Grandma's china set. Pauline also wanted it, and said, Dad told her she could have it. They were both so angry. I tried to stay out of the fray, but both looked to me to take sides. A decision had to be made, and as much as I hated doing it, I said the set should be divided. I thought that was pretty Solomonic, but can you believe now they're both angry—at me! Imagine—all of this over an old, beat-up set of china.

Tom

Drawbacks: First, just because you value only certain items does not mean that other items may not have value to your heirs. Unless you plan to itemize every item in your house, you may inadvertently omit the one item in dispute. Second, the list requires constant updating. If you buy something new or get rid of something, you could be in the same position as you were. Lots of squabbles begin over items that are on a list but no longer exist. If there is already potential for distrust (for example, a second marriage), it is easy to imagine accusations of theft. Finally, you may assign the master bedroom bureau to one child and the guest bedroom bureau to another child—exactly opposite of what they would have wanted. Sometimes, the mere act of reducing these items to writing inhibits beneficiaries from asking for an alternative distribution. After all, "if Dad wanted me to have this one, then I have to honor his wishes."

2. Tag items in the house with people's names now. We know several people who have done this and say it worked very well. If a child sees their name on something that child does not want, or missing from something the child does want, something can be said now.

    Drawbacks: First, if you change names around over time, someone whose name was once on the dining room table may accuse the new recipient of wrongdoing. Second, it may not be practical at age 30, 40, or 50 to label all of your assets anticipating your death.

3. Set up a system to draw lots. Drawing lots ensures each of the children has an opportunity to get what they want without letting emotions play a disproportionate role in the decision-making process. Some people suggest doing this room by room avoids the situation where one person selects a pair of cheap earrings and another person selects the entire living room set.

4. Design a system for resolving conflicts. Assuming you want the beneficiaries to decide among themselves, create a plan for what should happen in the event of a dispute. For example, leave the decision up to the executor or direct the executor to sell any disputed items and simply divide the proceeds.

No system is perfect; your goal can only be to try and head off any problems before they begin.

Learn the Language

Key Terms to Know When Paving the Way

de facto guardian guardian in fact, with or without a legal right

limited liability company (LLC) a creation of state law that provides liability protection for its owners and flexible tax treatment.

limited liability partnership (LLP) a creation of state law that provides some liability protection of business owners from their partners' misconduct.

Light the Path

What Your Heirs Need to Know

▶ Saying Good-bye: Fulfilling Your Final Wishes

One of the kindest things you can do for your family is to spare them needless frustrations and stressful decisions at the time of your death. Many people live together for 50 years without discussing their wishes regarding life support, organ donations, funeral or memorial services, burial, or cremation. Without intending to make a difficult time more difficult, they leave many distressing decisions for their loved ones. You can make your death easier on your family simply by deciding on and recording your own preferences (your will is not the best place for detailing such wishes, because it may not be read until after your burial), and, of course, discussing them with your family members.

Not only can writing down your wishes regarding your funeral arrangements make things easier for your loved ones immediately after your death, but, if you choose to do so, you can also make your own funeral arrangements. If you choose to go down this road, make sure you put the information in writing and that your executor and your spouse or unmarried partner know where these instructions are stored.

Before You Go: Planning Your Funeral

There's another reason to consider doing this in advance. Funerals and related items like burial plots, headstones, and so on can cost thousands of dollars and may, in fact, be the largest purchases your family ever makes, apart from your home and your children's education. The earlier you consider your options, the less likely it is that you will overspend or waste your money.

In your written instructions, indicate whether you want to be buried or cremated and whether you want to donate your organs. Also, describe your funeral or memorial service—who you want to speak, where it should be held, what music you want played, who to invite, and so on. If you have purchased a burial plot and arranged for a casket, record that information too.

If you are not careful, the cost of your funeral can add up quickly. For example, many funeral directors sell the entire funeral as a package, including items—such as pallbearers—that you and your family may not want. Obtain an itemized list of what the package includes and eliminate those you don't want. Also, investigate the full range of alternatives, from the least expensive casket to the most elaborate. Funeral directors can quote prices over the phone so you can comparison shop.

By opting for a prearranged funeral package, you can shop more calmly than your family can at your death, which should allow you to obtain a better deal than your survivors might. In addition, by researching and choosing among the various burial options, you know exactly what will happen to you after your death, and your family knows that your funeral will be conducted according to your wishes.

You can arrange your own funeral so your family will not have to raise the funds to cover your burial when they are least capable of doing so. This can be done with or without prepaying. Since funeral competition is heating up and prices in some areas going down, prepaying may not be the best plan. Consider a Totten Trust—an individual savings plan earmarked for your funeral. While you live, you control the money, which is usually invested in a certificate of deposit or a money-market account. When you die, the funds are available immediately to pay for your funeral.

Another such fund is a regulated trust, in which your money is invested by the funeral home or cemetery to pay for your burial. You have no access to this money. This trust is enormously profitable for the funeral home or cemetery because it keeps the earnings that your capital generates after you die if your funeral costs less than the funds you deposited. The best prearranged packages will refund any unused money to your estate.

Before you sign up for a pre-funded funeral, find out whether you can get a total or partial refund if you change your mind about the package. For example, if you move, you might want to be buried in another state. Or you might not have the money to make your installment payments and want a refund of what you have already paid. Also learn whether your current payment protects you against future price increases for funerals and related services. Most policies do, but make sure that yours is one of them. In addition, find out what happens if the funeral home you are dealing with goes out of business. Normally, its contracts will be transferred to another home, but you should know which home that might be.

One way to defray the high cost of funeral services is to join a local funeral consumer group once known as a memorial society. These organizations, which act as consumer advocates for funeral planning, are nonprofit, voluntary associations of people from all walks of life who support consumer choice for dignified, meaningful, affordable funerals.

Local societies can guide you to more affordable burial alternatives in your hometown. For example, it might not be necessary to use a funeral home to conduct a burial in your state. In other cases, memorial societies make arrangements with local undertakers to provide inexpensive funerals at a preset cost for members. When you join, you will be sent a prearrangement form allowing you to choose burial, cremation, or donation. You can also describe the kind of service you want.

Educated funeral consumers get more for their funeral dollars and usually spend less. To find a nonprofit consumer group near you, call Funeral Consumers Alliance at 800-765-0107 or visit its Web site at http://www.funerals.org.

The Gift of Life: Organ Donation

Whatever method of disposition or type of funeral you choose, you can also donate your organs to a person in need or your body to medical science.

If you decide to donate, you can indicate which organs to donate. The donor recipients pay for any costs incurred for removing the organs, but you are financially responsible for how you want your body to be taken care of after the organ donation. Many states will mark your driver's license if you are an organ donor.

Experimentation performed on cadavers is extremely important to the advancement of medical research, and many people feel that they make a significant contribution by offering their body to science. In some cases, the medical schools will pay to transport the body; in other cases, your estate must pay the bill.

Clearly, the decisions on whether to donate your organs to people in need and/or your body to medical research should be made calmly and well in advance of your death.

Make sure your family knows about your wishes and agrees to them.

▶ Travelogue: Where to Find Important Documents

Many wills simply divide estates into bulk portions, mentioning major assets but leaving heirs, executors, and the courts to determine the remaining contents of the deceased's estate. Without clear records, the family is faced with the burdensome and often costly task of locating records, papers, and documents to establish the content and value of the estate. Furthermore, certain major assets are not even typically included in wills. Life insurance proceeds, pensions, Social Security, and veteran's benefits, for example, all have fixed plans of distribution unaffected by wills, and so they are not commonly mentioned in them. Therefore, a clear, up-to-date, comprehensive listing of all your available assets and your benefits can be invaluable to your heirs. What to Pack: Where to Find Records and Keys offers an easy-to-prepare form that will be an invaluable guide for your loved ones. One important reminder: Don't forget to update it as things change.

▶ Souvenirs: Your Personal History

Perhaps the most cherished legacy you can provide your heirs is your unique knowledge of your family history, your recollections about your own life, interests, and accomplishments, and other special remembrances. You can write it down or make a cassette or CD; you might even decide to make a video of yourself. Other family members might want to participate and ask you questions. However you do it, we strongly suggest you do it.

After all, no one knows your personal history as well as you do. Do your children know where you were born? Where you went to school? In what cities you have lived? Your mother's family name? Where your parents lived or are

What to Pack

Where to Find Records and Keys

Personal History	Other Locations

Safe-Deposit Box

▶ Adoption papers
▶ Annulment decrees or judgments
▶ Athletic awards
▶ Birth certificates
▶ Change of name certificates
▶ Civic awards
▶ Death certificates
▶ Divorce decrees or judgments
▶ Dramatic awards
▶ Educational certificates
▶ Educational transcripts
▶ Marriage certificates
▶ Military awards
▶ Military separation papers
▶ Naturalization papers
▶ Newspaper articles
▶ Organization awards
▶ Organization membership certificates
▶ Other _____
  _____
  _____

Insurance

▶ Life insurance policies
▶ Medical and health insurance policies
▶ Residence insurance policies
▶ Vehicle insurance policies
▶ Other _____
  _____
  _____

Other Benefits

▶ 401(k) agreements
▶ IRA agreements
▶ Keogh plan agreements
▶ Medicare card

Personal History	Other Locations

Other Benefits (continued)

▶ Military separation papers _____

▶ Pension agreements _____

▶ Railroad retirement documents _____

▶ Social Security card _____

▶ Workers' compensation award _____

▶ Other _____ _____

_____ _____

_____ _____

Banking and Savings

▶ Cash _____

▶ Checking account statements _____

▶ Credit union account statements _____

▶ Savings account books or statements _____

▶ Other _____ _____

_____ _____

_____ _____

Securities, Real Estate, and Miscellaneous Assets

▶ Business records _____

▶ Decrees _____

▶ Deeds _____

▶ Home improvement records _____

▶ Judgments _____

▶ Leases _____

▶ Mortgages _____

▶ Patents or copyrights _____

▶ Rental property records _____

▶ Stock brokerage statements _____

▶ Vehicle certificates of title _____

▶ Other _____ _____

_____ _____

_____ _____

Will, Trust Agreements, Etc.

▶ Living will _____

▶ Powers of attorney _____

▶ Durable power of attorney for financial management _____

▶ Durable power of attorney for health care _____

▶ Other powers of attorney _____

▶ Trust agreement _____

► Will and codicils

► Other _____

_____

_____

Final Wishes

► Body bequeathal papers

► Cemetery deed

► Funeral prearrangement agreement

► Funeral prepayment agreement

► Mausoleum deed

► Uniform donor card

► Other _____

_____

_____

Miscellaneous Information

► Animal care information

► Burglar alarm information

► Child care information

► Letters to be sent upon my death

► List of hiding places for valuables

► Property care information

► Tax records

► Other _____

_____

_____

Keys and Combinations

► Keys to homes

► Keys to other real estate

► Keys to post office boxes

► Keys to safe-deposit box(es)

► Keys to vehicles

► Other keys

► List of combinations to locks

Other

► Passcode to online service(s)

► Cassettes

► Computer and other electronic media

► Photos

► Videos/movies

► Other _____

_____

_____

buried? The different types of work experiences you have had? The hobbies and clubs you have enjoyed through the years? Probably not.

And yet, haven't you asked yourself many of these questions about your own parents? Or your grandparents? Or your brothers and sisters? Most of us become more interested in family history as we age, but if someone does not record the facts of that history for us, they will be lost. You are the one who can do this best for your heirs.

Telephone, drop a note, or e-mail your parent, brother, sister, aunt, uncle, son, or daughter and gradually complete your personal history. As a bonus, you might even rekindle family ties!

▶ Travel Checklist

Review the following list periodically and discuss any shortcomings you find with your professional financial, tax, and legal advisors.

1. Do you have a written estate plan?

   - ▶ Do you understand it?
   - ▶ Has it been reviewed within the past three years?
   - ▶ Does it include an analysis of all potential strategies?
   - ▶ Did you fully implement the selected strategies?

2. Do you have a will?

   - ▶ Has it been reviewed within the past three years?
   - ▶ Was it updated when you moved to a new state, got married or divorced, had a baby, lost a parent, or experienced any other significant family change?
   - ▶ Does your will name a guardian for your children if both you and your spouse die?
   - ▶ Does your will create a trust (and name a trustee) to control assets for minor children if both you and your spouse die?
   - ▶ Have you made appropriate provisions for any children with special needs?
   - ▶ Are you comfortable with the executor(s) and trustee(s) you selected?

3. Have you considered a living trust to avoid probate?

   ▶ If you have a living trust, have you retitled your assets in the name of that trust?

4. Have you delegated appropriate powers of attorney so that, in the event of your mental or physical incompetence, your affairs can be managed by people you choose?

5. Are you taking full advantage of the marital deduction?

   ▶ Have you retitled assets in the name of this trust?

6. Have you set up irrevocable life insurance trusts to ensure your life insurance proceeds are not taxed as part of your estate?

   ▶ Did you retitle existing life insurance policies into the trust?
   ▶ Is the amount of insurance in the trust sufficient to pay estimated taxes and transfer costs due at your death? Have you reviewed this estimate within the last three years?
   ▶ If you need to add more insurance to the trust, have you done so?
   ▶ Are you routinely sending out any required "Crummey" letters for these trusts?

7. Are you taking maximum advantage of the $11,000 annual gift tax exclusions?

   ▶ Have you considered annual gifts to your children and grandchildren?
   ▶ If so, do you make them outright gifts or gifts to a trust for their benefit?

8. Are you taking maximum advantage of medical and education gift tax exclusions?

   ▶ Do you have grandchildren in college (or private/parochial elementary or high schools) who could use help with their tuition?
   ▶ Do you have parents or grandparents in hospitals or nursing homes who could use help with their medical bills?

9. If you have highly appreciated assets that don't generate current income, have you considered using them to fund a charitable remainder trust?

10. If you are a sole proprietor, a partner, or an owner of a closely held corporation:

> ▶ Do you have a buy-sell agreement for the business?
> ▶ Have you considered key person life and disability coverage?
> ▶ Is there a written business continuation plan?

The bottom line: If you have taken the time to create a net worth, you need to complete the process by careful and skillful transition planning. Make sure your money goes to the people and causes you care about—in a time and manner you choose!

Appendix A

An Itinerary

Here's a quick review of what to do, as you set out on the road to planning your estate.

Stop # 1. Good estate planning settles not only the disposition of possessions and money but also other major life decisions, including custody of children. For this reason, you are never too poor or too young to have an estate plan.

- ▶ Estate planning is a process, not a product. It involves seeking advice, reviewing options, and creating a plan for ensuring that your assets are sufficient to meet your objectives for your heirs; your heirs receive those assets in the proportion, manner, and timeframe you choose; income, estate, gift, inheritance taxes, and transfer costs are minimized; and that liquidity exists to pay taxes and transfer costs when they are due.
- ▶ Things to consider: who gets how much of your money and possessions; how to give away assets as tax-free gifts while you live to minimize estate taxes when you die; who to name as a guardian for your children, trustee to administer any trusts you may establish, and executor of your estate; what advance directives you wish to make about health care as well as what you want done with your body after you die.
- ▶ Begin by creating a detailed inventory of your assets and liabilities (see Roadmap 1.1).
- ▶ Determine the type of documents you will need; for example, will, revocable living trust, power of attorney, medical documents, living will, durable power of attorney for health care.
- ▶ Decide whether you will do it yourself or if you will need an attorney and/or tax advisor before proceeding. Do you need a financial planner, insurance agent, and your accountant?

Stop # 2. If a will is part of your estate plan, it will provide directions on how you want your assets distributed as well as who will be in charge of distributing them to your heirs.

▶ Determine what should and should not be included in your will. A will covers both tangible assets, like homes, cars, boats, artwork, collectibles, and furniture, as well as intangible assets, like bank accounts, stocks, bonds, and mutual funds. Other rights and benefits, like any trusts you might establish, pension rights and life insurance proceeds, are normally handled outside of your will.

▶ Determine who your beneficiaries will be, what you intend to leave to each of them, and whether or not they have special needs that should be addressed in your will. If they are minors, at what age should they inherit and how are they to be taken care of (both financially and physically) while they are minors? If you have children from more than one marriage or out of wedlock or are divorced, determine how they should be treated. Pets? Charities? Friends? All can be addressed in your will if you wish them to inherit money or personal property or be cared for after you die.

▶ Familiarize yourself with the duties and responsibilities of an executor, the pros and cons of having a professional executor vs. a friend or family member (you can have both or more than one of either), and decide who will be the executor(s) of your will.

▶ If you are working with an attorney, put together all the documentation you will need to prepare the will efficiently, to avoid unnecessary legal fees, and to make certain you have not forgotten anything.

▶ Don't forget a living will and health care power of attorney; draw these up at the same time as you prepare your will. If you wish to donate organs, make that wish known to your family and the person to whom you give your health care power of attorney.

▶ Review your will periodically to ensure that it continues to reflect the assets you own and your wishes for what will happen to them after you die, and to make sure that it continues to reflect your current family situation.

Stop # 3. The primary goals of estate planning are (1) to ensure that as much of your estate as possible goes to your beneficiaries and is not depleted by probate, taxes, and other expenses; (2) to ensure that your estate transfers to your beneficiaries as quickly as possible.

▶ You can minimize costs by carefully planning your estate and by writing a legally valid and clearly worded will, selecting a competent executor (who may be able to do some of the work of an attorney), and passing as much of your estate as possible outside your will.

▶ Consider the following options for passing your assets outside your will: (1) own as many assets as possible as a joint tenant with right of survivorship; (2) own assets with your spouse as a tenant by the entirety; (3) name beneficiaries to your life insurance policy, employee benefits plan, and/or IRA; (4) give assets away as gifts while you are alive; (5) set up informal trust accounts; and (6) establish a living trust.

▶ If probate is a concern, focus on reducing the assets in your estate that will go through probate.

▶ If estate taxes are an issue, minimize the size of your taxable estate.

▶ If your estate is small enough, ensure that it qualifies for the quicker and cheaper alternatives to probate that may be available in your state.

▶ Each estate planning instrument has its own advantages and disadvantages; examine them thoroughly to determine which are right for your situation. Roadmap 3.1 offers a handy summary.

Stop # 4. Trusts are the primary estate planning tools used to avoid probate; chosen correctly they also offer great flexibility and give you the greatest amount of control over the assets you leave to a beneficiary, even after you die.

▶ Like a will, a trust requires a formal, written, legal document. Although you can create a trust agreement on your own, have it reviewed by an estate planning attorney. If it is complicated, don't do it yourself—the amount of money you save today may cost your heirs even more tomorrow. A trust document is valid only when set up correctly.

▶ Before establishing a trust or trusts, determine your goals; different trusts are best for achieving different ends; learn the differences among informal bank trusts, testamentary trusts, and living (inter vivos) trusts and between revocable and irrevocable trusts.

▶ Trusts should not necessarily hold every asset. For example, it is unwise to deposit the stock of a closely held corporation or stock options in a trust.

▶ Carefully select a trustee. If you have both a will and a trust(s), the executor and the trustee(s) do not have to be the same people.

▶ Before establishing a trust, weigh its benefits against its costs and then compare them to the costs and benefits of other estate planning tools available to you.

Stop # 5. Life insurance is not just for the breadwinner, and is an important part of planning for your heirs.

▶ Calculate how much life insurance your heirs need. The funds should be enough to replace your paycheck or to cover the cost of having someone provide the services you now provide, cover daily living expenses, and pay your final medical bills and burial costs. In addition, the insurance proceeds should provide income for long-term needs such as retirement, estate taxes, or college costs. Roadmaps 5.1 and 5.2 will help you estimate these expenses as well as your heirs' anticipated income.

▶ Understand the different types of life insurance—term, whole life, universal life, and variable life—and annuities—fixed and variable—available to you to determine which is appropriate to your situation.

▶ Once you know what you need, shop around. Watch out for high fees and expenses, cancellation fees, or surrender charges, and use the interest-adjusted net cost index to help you make your final decision. Last, but not least, investigate the company—will it be around when it's time to pay off?

▶ If you own a business, investigate the role disability and life insurance can play in protecting it if you suffer a long-term illness and when you die.

▶ Not everyone is entitled to survivor's benefits; however, in computing your family's income, don't forget about Social Security and veteran's benefits.

▶ Pensions, IRAs and other benefit plans will augment other sources of income, and, depending on your family's immediate needs, may be a way to build capital. These plans are complex; therefore, understand your plans and the impact of your decisions.

Stop # 6. Protecting your family involves more than sound financial planning. Who, for example, should be named as the guardian of your minor child? How do you provide for adopted children; children from previous marriages, or out-of-wedlock children? What about your new spouse (blended families have a unique set of issues)? How should you dispose of your business—keep it in the family or sell it? And, what about your personal possessions?

▶ Name a guardian and alternate guardian for minor children in your will. If you do not, and you and your spouse die, the court will appoint a guardian, who may or may not be the person you'd choose. (If one parent dies, custody usually goes to the spouse, the child's surviving legal or biological parent, regardless of whether you are divorced or separated.)

▶ Provide financially for your children. You have many options; their advantages and disadvantages are outlined in Roadmap 6.1.

▶ If you have a minor or adult child with special needs, consider options for long-term care and guardianship; write a letter of intent describing your expectations; and consider a "special needs trust."

▶ Provide for your spouse and your adult children using the many methods available, but take special precautions when yours is a blended family; consider for example a prenuptial agreement, make sure title to all assets have been appropriately transferred, etc.

▶ What do you want to have happen to your business after you die? Your options include selling it, passing it on to one or more of your family members to own and run, or liquidating its assets. Whatever your decision, all require careful planning and preparation, and should be discussed with your family as well as an attorney versed in business estate planning.

▶ Set up a system for the division of your personal possessions—large and small, expensive or not—it's often arguments over these that sour family relationships.

Stop # 7. Your estate plan is almost complete, but before it's finished, there are some important decisions to be made.

▶ Discuss your wishes regarding life support, organ donations, funeral or memorial services, burial, or cremation with your family. Put those wishes in writing and make sure your family and your executor know where to find them.

▶ Consider pre-arranging your funeral; while it's not a pleasant thing to think about, it will save your family much stress during a difficult time and could also save money.

▶ Create and periodically review and update a list telling your family and executor where they can find important documents.

▶ Think about creating a family history for your family—write it, record it, tape it—whatever method you use, it will be a souvenir your family and their families will enjoy.

▶ Last but not least, review your estate plan regularly and update anything in it that needs to be changed. Estate planning isn't easy, but it can give you peace of mind to know that the people you love will be well cared for when you can't care for them yourself.

Bon voyage!

Appendix B

The Best of *Planning an Estate*: A Resource Guide

▶ Bibliography

The following books were used as resources for this book. In addition, we have provided lists of other books and Web sites that offer more detailed information on some of the topics covered in this book. We hope you find all these resources useful.

Barney, Colleen, Esq. and Victoria Collins, Ph.D., CFP. *Best Intentions.* Chicago: Dearborn Trade Publishing, 2002.

Bronchick, William. *Wealth Protection Secrets of a Millionaire Real Estate Investor.* Dearborn Trade Publishing, 2003.

Cohn, Mike with Jayne Pearl. *Keep or Sell your Business ... How to Make the Decision Every Private Company Faces.* Dearborn Trade Publishing, 2001.

Downing, Neil. *The New IRAs and How to Make Them Work for You.* Dearborn Trade Publishing, 2002.

Garrett, Sheryl, CFP. *Just Give Me the Answers.* Dearborn Trade Publishing, 2004.

Goodman, Jordan E. *Everyone's Money Book,* 3rd Ed. Chicago: Dearborn Trade Publishing, 2001.

Lewis, Allyson, CFP. *The Million Dollar Car and $250,000 Pizza.* Dearborn Trade Publishing, 2000.

Magee, David S. and John Ventura. *Everything Your Heirs Need to Know.* Chicago: Dearborn Trade Publishing, 1999.

Ventura, John. *The Will Kit,* 2nd Ed. Chicago: Dearborn Trade Publishing, 2002.

▶ Recommended Books and Web Sites

For Chapter 1, Design Your Itinerary
Books

▶ *Beyond the Grave: The Right Way and the Wrong Way of Leaving Money to Your Children (And Others)* by Gerald M. Condon and Jeffrey L. Condon (HarperBusiness, P.O. Box 588, Dunmore, PA 18512; Telephone: 212-207-7000; 800-331-3761; http://www.harpercollins.com). Explains how to provide fairly and equitably for family members, facilitate charitable bequests, avoid probate, and prevent conflict and preserve family relationships.

▶ *The Complete Book of Wills, Estates & Trusts* by Alexander A. Bove (Henry Holt and Co., 115 W. 18th St., New York, NY 10011; Telephone: 212-886-9200; http://www.henryholt.com). Details the most up-to-date laws and benefits for a variety of trusts.

▶ *The Complete Idiot's Guide to Wills and Estates* by Stephen M. Maple (Macmillan Publishing, 866 Third Ave., New York, NY 10022; Telephone: 212-702-2000; http://www.macmillan.com). Lays out a whole process, including step-by-step directions for writing a will, language to be used in letters to executors and heirs, and power of attorney.

▶ *Death & Taxes: The Complete Guide to Family Inheritance Planning* by Randell C. Doane and Rebecca G. Doane (Ohio University Press, Scott Quadrangle, Athens, OH 45701; Telephone: 740-593-1158; http://www.ohiou.edu).

▶ *Estate Planning* by Martin M. Shenkman (Barron's Educational Series, 250 Wireless Blvd., Hauppauge, NY 11788; Telephone: 631-434-3311; 800-645-3476; http://www.barronseduc.com). A guide to all the legal and tax aspects and financial details of estate planning.

▶ *Estate Planning Made Easy* by David T. Phillips and Bill S. Wolfkiel (Dearborn Trade, 155 N. Wacker Dr., Chicago, IL 60606; Telephone: 312-836-4400; 800-245-2665; http://www.dearborntrade.com). Offers the basics of estate planning and shows the advantages of early estate planning.

▶ *Plan Your Estate: Absolutely Everything You Need to Know to Protect Your Loved Ones* by Denis Clifford and Cora Jordan (Nolo Press, 950 Parker St., Berkeley, CA 94710; Telephone: 800-992-6656; http://www.nolo.com). Deals with many issues related to planning an estate: children and probate; estate and gift taxes; second marriages and a variety of trust options; married people vs. single; joint tenancy; life insurance; retirement benefits; taxes; organ donations and types of beneficiaries; and wills.

Web sites

▶ EstateWeb.com. This site specializes in estate-planning issues and offers a basic estate tax estimator that will give you a quick general snapshot of what your heirs can expect to pay. http://www.estateweb.com

▶ Nolo.com. The legal do-it-yourself publishing company's site provides entries from a law encyclopedia that explains estate planning in plain English. http://www.nolo.com

For Chapter 2, Map Your Trip

Books

▶ *The Complete Will Kit* by Jens C. Appel III (John Wiley & Sons Inc., 10475 Crosspoint Blvd. Indianapolis, IN 46256; Telephone: 877 762-2974, http://www.wiley.com). Contains all the forms you need to write a will, as well as state-by-state legal requirements for wills.

▶ *How to Make Your Own Will* by Mark Warda (Sourcebooks, P.O. Box 4410, Naperville, IL 60567; Telephone: 630-961-3900; 800-432-7444; http://www.sourcebooks.com). A self-help law kit with forms.

▶ *Nolo's Will Book* by Denis Clifford (Nolo Press, 950 Parker St., Berkeley, CA 94710; Telephone: 510-549-1976; 800-992-NOLO; 800-992-6656; http://www.nolo.com). Explains why you need a will and shows you what the will must cover to be legally valid. Discusses guardianship, creating trusts, and avoiding probate. Also comes with a floppy disk with will forms.

Web sites

▶ Will Works. This is a simple will-making site with the proper questions and forms that allow you to think through and write your will. http://www.willworks.com

Software

▶ WillMaker (Nolo Press, 950 Parker St., Berkeley, CA 94710; Telephone: 510-549-1976; 800-992-NOLO; 800-992-6656; http://www.nolo.com). Leads you step-by-step through the process of writing a will; helps you establish testamentary and other types of trusts. Includes a living will or health care directives module allowing you to specify what kinds of health care you want provided or withheld in the event you cannot communicate your wishes. Also includes funeral planning and burial arrangement documents.

For Chapter 3, Negotiate Customs
Books

▶ *8 Ways to Avoid Probate* by Mary Randolph (Nolo Press, 950 Parker St., Berkeley, CA 94710; Telephone: 800-992-6656; http://www.nolo.com). Explanation of probate avoidance techniques.

▶ *9 Ways to Avoid Estate Taxes* by Mary Randolph and Denis Clifford (Nolo Press, 950 Parker St., Berkeley, CA 94710; Telephone: 800-992-6656; http://www.nolo.com). Presents nine major methods people can use to avoid or reduce federal estate taxes.

▶ *Probate and Settling an Estate* by James John Jurinski (Barron's Educational Series, 250 Wireless Blvd., Hauppauge, NY 11788; Telephone: 631-434-3311; 800-645-3476; http://www.barronseduc.com). A review of the probate process, the executor's role, details of probate, understanding a will's provisions, managing property, paying creditors and taxes, closing an estate, and dealing with special problems.

For Chapter 4, Choose Your Vehicle
Books

▶ *The Complete Book of Trusts* by Martin M. Shenkman (John Wiley & Sons Inc., 10475 Crosspoint Blvd. Indianapolis, IN 46256; Telephone: 877-762-2974, http://www.wiley.com). How to set up a trust to manage assets in the event of disability or death, avoid probate, secure assets from Medicaid and creditors, and minimize estate and other transfer taxes.

▶ *How to Settle a Living Trust: How You Can Settle a Living Trust Swiftly, Easily, and Safely* by Henry W. Abts (Contemporary Books, Wright Group/McGraw-Hill, 220 East Danieldale Rd., DeSoto, TX 75115-2490; Telephone: 800-621-1918; http://www.mhcontemporarybooks.com). This guide provides information on how to dissolve and dispose of assets and understand legal and financial aspects of trusts.

▶ *Introduction to Trusts* (Dearborn Trade, 155 N. Wacker Dr., Chicago, IL 60606; Telephone: 312-836-4400; 800-245-2665; http://www.dearborn trade.com)

▶ *Make Your Own Living Trust* by Denis Clifford (Nolo Press, 950 Parker St., Berkeley, CA 94710; Telephone: 510-549-1976; 800-992-NOLO; 800-992-6656; http://www.nolo.com). Explains the living trust—how it works, how property is transferred to the trust, when you need one, and how to create one. It also provides all the tear-out forms and instructions necessary to create a basic living trust, a marital life estate trust, and a back-up will.

Software

▶ *Living TrustMaker* (Nolo Press, 950 Parker St., Berkeley, CA 94710; Telephone: 510-549-1976; 800-992-NOLO; 800-992-6656; http://www.nolo. com). Designed to help non-lawyers write a revocable living trust to avoid probate and transfer property to heirs safely and quickly while avoiding legal fees.

For Chapter 5, Travel Insurance

Books

▶ *Building Your Future with Annuities: A Consumer's Guide* (Consumer Information Center, Pueblo, CO 81009; Telephone: 719-948-3334; http:// www.pueblo.gsa.gov). A free brochure from Fidelity Investments that explains various types of annuities and how they should be used. Can also be obtained directly from Fidelity; Telephone: 800-544-2442.

▶ *Buying Insurance* by Stuart Schwartz and Craig Conley (Capstone Press, P.O. Box 669, Mankato, MN 56002; Telephone: 800-747-4992; http://www. capstone-press.com)

▶ *The Complete Guide to Long-Term Care Insurance* by Robert W. Davis (Long-Term Care Quote, 600 W. Ray Road, Suite D4, Chandler, AZ 85224; Telephone: 602-899-9983; 800-587-3279; http://www.longtermcarequote. com). A comprehensive guide to long-term care insurance. Includes extensive analyses of costs related to long-term care, including costs of care in every state.

▶ *How to Insure Your Life: A Step by Step Guide to Buying the Coverage You Need at Prices You Can Afford* by Reg Wilson and the Silver Lake editors (Silver Lake Publishing, 2025 Hyperion Ave., Los Angeles, CA

90027; Telephone: 323-663-3084; 888-663-3091; http://www.silverlakepub. com). Provides tips and tactics to help people get the best life insurance coverage for their money. Includes easy-to-use forms.

▶ *The Complete Idiot's Guide to Buying Insurance and Annuities* by Brian H. Breuel (John Wiley & Sons Inc., 10475 Crosspoint Blvd. Indianapolis, IN 46256; Telephone: 877-762-2974, http://www.wiley.com). Provides simple explanations and illustrations to help the reader understand insurance jargon and includes tips to advise the reader on insurance and annuity matters.

▶ *Life Insurance: A Consumer's Handbook* by Joseph M. Belth (Indiana University Press, 601 N. Morton St., Bloomington, IN 47404; Telephone: 812-855-6804; 800-842-6796; http://www.iupress.indiana.org). A systematic explanation of personal insurable risk and how to transfer that risk to an insurance company, and strategies for assessing how good your policy is.

▶ *Life Insurance Boot Camp Buyer's Guide* by William Brownlie (Life Insurance Boot Camp, 87 Parkhurst Dr., P.O. Box 441, Westford, MA 01886; http://www.lifeinsurancebootcamp.com). Complete coverage of the various types of life insurance, and how to decide which policy and company is right for you; includes information on disability and long-term health care insurance.

For Chapter 6, Paving The Way
Books

▶ *Caring for the Dead: Your Final Act of Love* by Lisa Carlson (Upper Access Press, P.O. Box 457, Hinesburg, VT 05461; Telephone: 800-356-9315). A comprehensive guide to arranging a low-cost but dignified funeral, written by the executive director of the Funeral and Memorial Societies of America. Also lists all the laws pertaining to the funeral industry in every state in America.

For Chapter 7, Light The Path
Web sites

▶ Aging with Dignity. Features "Five Wishes," which includes templates for several types of living wills and conforms with the law in 33 states and the District of Columbia. http://www.agingwithdignity.org

Index

Page numbers shown in *italic* indicate references to a Roadmap, Tollbooth, or What to Pack feature.

Notes

Notes

Notes

Notes